WOMEN AND MEDIA

Other Titles of Interest

BAUER, C. and RITT, L.
Free and Ennobled: Source Readings in the Development of Victorian Feminism

HERRMANN, E. R. and SPITZ, E. H.
German Women Writers of the Twentieth Century

NELSON, N.
Why Has Development Neglected Rural Women?

SHAFFER, H. G.
Women in the Two Germanies: A Comparative Study of a Socialist and a Non-Socialist Society

STEWART, D. W.
The Women's Movement in Community Politics: The Role of Local Commissions on the Status of Women

NEWMARK, E.
Women's Roles: A Cross-cultural Perspective

WOMEN AND MEDIA

Edited by

Helen Baehr

PERGAMON PRESS

OXFORD · NEW YORK · TORONTO · SYDNEY · PARIS · FRANKFURT

U.K.	Pergamon Press Ltd., Headington Hill Hall, Oxford OX3 0BW, England
U.S.A.	Pergamon Press Inc., Maxwell House, Fairview Park, Elmsford, New York 10523, U.S.A.
CANADA	Pergamon of Canada, Suite 104, 150 Consumers Road, Willowdale, Ontario M2J 1P9, Canada
AUSTRALIA	Pergamon Press (Aust.) Pty. Ltd., P.O. Box 544, Potts Point, N.S.W. 2011, Australia
FRANCE	Pergamon Press SARL, 24 rue des Ecoles, 75240 Paris, Cedex 05, France
FEDERAL REPUBLIC OF GERMANY	Pergamon Press GmbH, 6242 Kronberg-Taunus, Hammerweg 6, Federal Republic of Germany

British Library Cataloguing in Publication Data
Women and media.
1. Women in mass media.
I. Baehr, Helen
II. 'Women's studies international quarterly'
301.16'1   P96.H6   80-41424
ISBN 0 08 026061 6

Published as Volume 3, Number 1, of the Journal *Women's Studies International Quarterly* and supplied to subscribers as part of their subscription. Also available to non-subscribers.

Printed in Great Britain by A. Wheaton & Co. Ltd., Exeter

EDITORIAL

The contents of any journal are bound, by the very nature and purpose of the beast, to be eclectic. The articles contained here are no exception. They range across a number of varied theoretical and empirical approaches to the study of women and the mass media. A good deal of important work is being done elsewhere on feminist film theory and practice and, for this reason only, film is not covered in the main articles here.

From its very beginnings the Women's Liberation Movement has responded critically, often angrily, to women's—and its own—representation in the mass media. This pressure, along with a growing involvement by feminists studying and teaching Media and Women's Studies, has opened up the whole question of the special nature of women's relationship to the media.

It has always struck me how relatively neglected the subject of women and broadcasting has been in the growing volume of research and debate. One reason for this—in Britain anyway—may lie in the difficulty of access to programmes. It is almost impossible here, with copyright legislation as it stands, to see television programmes (legally) more than once, i.e. at their time of transmission. This restriction may be lifted on educational programmes only after special negotiation with the copyright holders and erects an effective barrier to detailed studies of programme content. I am pleased that the articles on radio and television in this issue go some way towards filling that gap.

The mass media have been quick to respond to women as a new growth industry. The "liberated woman" stereotype holds as much potential for being a profitable consumer as the "traditional homemaker" image of the 1950s. The urgent need to consider seriously the problems and issues surrounding that reconstruction and representation of feminism and feminist issues within the patriarchal discourse of the mass media is one of the key themes addressed here.

The articles included discuss the twin areas of the employment and representation of women. Yet more work needs to be done to bring together the correspondences between women working in the media and the representations produced. We neglect making these connections at our peril. There is all the difference in the world between encouraging more women to become media professionals—"window-dressing the set"—and organising a real feminist challenge against media structures and "professional" practices which reproduce the subordinate role of women. The struggle against representation is basically the struggle against the structures of patriarchal economic and social relations which produce sexist media images and representations. For feminists working in the media this means fighting to develop alternative forms of organisation, production, distribution and consumption which are opposed to present conditions and dominant representations.

This collection reflects fairly accurately the current "state of the art". I welcome, and would like to encourage, more contributions from women working in the media industry who can offer insights and knowledge based on a practical experience not generally available to academics. I thank all the contributors for their hard work and co-operation and my friends for their support. It remains for the readers to judge what state the art is in.

HELEN BAEHR

CONTENTS

REPORTS

BOOK REVIEWS

Women's Studies Int. Quart., 1980, Vol. 3, pp. 1–13
© Pergamon Press Ltd.   Printed in Great Britain

0148–0685/80/0301–0001/$02.00/0

WOMEN IN BROADCASTING (U.S.)

*DE JURE, DE FACTO**

BARBARA MURRAY EDDINGS

Alfred I. DuPont-Columbia University Survey of Broadcast Journalism,
Columbia University, New York, NY 10027, U.S.A.

(*Accepted March* 1979)

'There can be no doubt our nation has a long and unfortunate history of sex discrimination. Traditionally, such discrimination was rationalized by an attitude of romantic paternalism which, in practical effect, put women not on a pedestal but in a cage. . . .'

> William J. Brennan, Jr.
> Frontiero vs Richardson 1971
> U.S. Supreme Court.

'Baby' HAS indeed come a long way since 1972, when the DuPont-Columbia Survey of Broadcast Journalism called station WSNS Chicago to task for having newscaster Linda Fuoco deliver the evening news from her sponsor's heart-shaped bed. 'Baby' may no longer be in the bedroom, but neither is she in the boardroom, although she has ceased to be a curiosity in the newsroom.

While women are entering the job market in ever-increasing numbers,[1] of the 449,000 Americans earning more than $25,000 annually, only 2·4 per cent are women. When *Broadcasting* magazine in June 1977 published top-level salaries of sixteen corporate directors and officers in communications, only one woman, Katherine Graham of the Washington Post Company, was on this very exclusive list.

Eight years have passed since the FCC, responding in 1971 to the repeated petitions of the National Organization for Women and the United Church of Christ, decided to include women in its affirmative action program for broadcasting. In those 8 years the biggest proportionate gains for any job category have been recorded by women newscasters, with television's commitment exceeding that of radio. Almost 90 per cent of the TV stations and 72 per cent of the radio stations reporting to the Du Pont Survey in 1977 said they employed women newscasters. More than half of the TV stations and one-third of the radio stations had women producers. Yet while women are making gains on the air and in the credits, the DuPont-Columbia correspondents, our cross-country network of local monitors, estimate only one in five of on-air reporters and producers is a woman.[2] Pam Hill, ABC producer, told the survey: 'Throughout the news division as a whole, the problem of having women

---

* This article is published by permission of the Trustees of Columbia University in the City of New York.
[1] U.S. Bureau of Labor statistics report that women, 53 per cent of the population, hold 41 per cent of the jobs, a doubling over the last 25 years.
[2] In network TV, *Time* magazine in March 1977 reported women constitute 13 per cent of all on-camera news gatherers.

in the highly visible jobs, on camera, but not in the real decision-making, producer and executive level jobs, continues.'

In top management the Survey figures mirror this concern. Only 3 per cent of the television stations and 2 per cent of the radio stations reporting to the survey had women as station or general managers. In 1975 and 1976 5 per cent of TV and radio stations had women news directors. In 1977 the figures remained unchanged in TV, although radio stations reported a 4 per cent increase over the previous year.

Writing in the Radio Television News Directors' Association's *Communicator* in March 1977, Ted Landphair, manager of news and public affairs at WMAL Radio in Washington, D.C., said:

'Great actresses and newswomen have emerged. Just enough to serve as carrots to the generation of idealistic young women who follow. Not until these women have tested the 'real world' do they feel the stick. Someone else, maybe committees of someone elses— usually male—manipulates their professional lives.'

Richard Wagner, WCHS-TV news director in Charleston, West Virginia, reported:

'I feel that at present there is still an atmosphere of discrimination against women in the media from men in the media who see them getting in easier than they did, from viewers who think all they are is a pretty face, and from management who look at them only as a statistic that needs to be filled in on an EEO form.'

The 1976 annual reports of the commercial and public networks are evidence of the dearth of women on the corporate level as well. ABC reported only one woman on its sixteen-member board, none on its executive committee, and only one in a list of twenty-four officers. On the CBS seventeen-member board, one is a woman; of twenty-two officers, one is a woman; and there are no women officers in the five-member CBS Broadcast Group listing. NBC, with thirteen members on its board of directors, had one woman; of ninety-seven officers, six are women. The Corporation for Public Broadcasting reported four women on its fifteen-member board,[3] and one of six executive officers is a woman. Of the Public Broadcasting Service board of thirty-three lay directors, six are women. There is one woman on its fifteen-member board of professionals, and neither of two management directors is a woman.

The Radio Television News Directors' Association for 1977 has no women officers, and of the fourteen regional directors none is a woman.[4]

Further, broadcasting's 'big brother,' the Federal Communications Commission, has had only three women commissioners since its inception in 1934. The two seats vacated in the fall of 1977 were both filled by men.

Commenting on the asymmetrical state of the industry, Marlene Sanders, former vice-president for ABC News and director of documentaries, told the Survey:

'I am the first woman in any network to be a VP in news, so while I'm doing all right,

---

[3] Since its inception in 1968, of the thirty-six board members, eight have been women. In October 1977 President Carter appointed two women, Sharon Percy Rockefeller and Gillian Sorensen, to succeed in seats vacated on the CPB board by two men, Thomas W. Moore and Robert Benjamin.

[4] At the 1977 RTNDA convention in San Francisco women members, piqued at being ignored by their male counterparts (no women on convention dais and no newswomen on panels), called a special study group to ensure representation at the 1978 convention.

lots of others aren't. . . . The net looks for experienced people in the first place and they have to get that experience out of New York, or at local stations. Women are hired in few numbers in those jobs and so there are too few qualified for middle management and above.'

Summer of 1977 found the industry in a defensive posture with the publication of the United States Civil Rights Commission report 'Window Dressing on the Set,' which charged that women and members of minority groups were almost totally excluded from decision-making positions in TV and that their actual employment status was misrepresented by the local stations. The news segment of the study covering commercial and public TV stations in the top forty markets during 1974–75 found that white males made 88.6 per cent of the monitored appearances of TV correspondents during that period and that most important stories were reported by men.

The first network to issue a denial was NBC, which charged that 'some of the commission's broad-brush charges appear to be based on out-of-date data and are not in accord with the facts, at least as they might concern NBC.'[5] Yet the network's news personnel listing, dated 1976 and updated in August 1977 for the Survey, lists only two women out of sixty-two managerial positions.

A former NBC woman producer of documentaries told the Survey: 'There is some visible progress in the lower ranks, minimal in the middle ranks, significant progress in on-the-air reporters, and none in management.' In the last year, she said, NBC has lost every senior newswoman—Barbara Walters, Lucy Jarvis, Christy Basham, and Joan Konner.

Executives at ABC responded to the Civil Rights Commission report by expressing confidence in their own organizational policies and claimed their practices 'are in full compliance with applicable federal laws and regulations.' Midge Kovacs, former ABC senior promotion writer, commented to the Survey: ' Each department is run by a man and each department has a few women with dead-ended positions. . . . The ABC experience has made me a corporate drop-out permanently.'

Bill Leonard, CBS vice-president for Washington, D.C., said that equality of opportunity is 'the very linchpin of CBS policy' and that 46 per cent of CBS employees are women. Leonard did not break down these figures according to importance of positions.[6] Ellen Erhlich, director of information services at CBS, told the Survey:

'As I go around the country, I see many more women in anchor positions and as reporters of hard news. I think the main area where we have not done as well is in top and middle management where the decisions are being made. We need more Marlene Sanderses.'

Broadcasters have, nevertheless, been pointing with pride to their top-level women. Walters's appointment to an ABC anchor position caused a media uproar in April 1976.

---

[5] Any change in the NBC track record, far from expressing independent action on the part of the net, was the result of a February 1977 $2 million out-of-court settlement of a sex-bias suit brought by women employees in December 1975. Under this agreement NBC was required to make 'good faith efforts' to promote women to a wide range of professional, managerial and official positions. Spelled out, the settlement called for a specific goal to include 15 per cent of the top NBC positions below the rank of vice-president as well as specific goals for hiring women to fill vacancies in technical jobs and news positions during the next 5 years.

[6] On November 8, 1977, Richard S. Salant, CBS News president, went on record to advocate preferential promotional treatment of blacks and women newscasters at his net 'until we get a better balance,' in a speech made to the North Carolina Associated Press Broadcasters Association annual meeting.

Less heralded, but tradition-breaking, was Lynn Scherr's appointment in the summer of
1976 as the first woman to serve as an anchor of a regularly scheduled prime time TV
network news series.[7]

As early as 1974 ABC broke tradition by naming Ann Compton to be the first woman
full-time network White House correspondent. Two years later NBC named Marilyn Berger
as its White House correspondent. Joining Compton and Berger and moving into areas
once considered all-male domains were Cassie Mackin (in 1972 she became the first woman
network TV floor reporter at a national political convention), Connie Chung, and Enid
Roth (who directed NBC's TV floor coverage during the convention), all prominent
figures at the 1976 political conventions. In September 1977 CBS promoted newswoman
Lesley Stahl to a Washington co-anchor spot on its 'Morning News,' replacing Bruce
Morton. And in October 1977 Charlayne Hunter-Gault, metropolitan reporter for the
New York Times, joined the MacNeil/Lehrer Report.

In management Marion Stephenson had become the first woman vice-president and
general manager in radio history with her appointment at NBC in May 1975. ABC promoted
Marlene Sanders in January 1976 to be the first woman network vice-president for TV
news. In September 1976 Susan Harmon was elected chairperson of the National Public
Radio board of directors. In January 1977 Ann Berk became the first woman station
manager for a network-owned station with her promotion at NBC's flagship station,
WNBC-TV New York. In June 1977 Jo Moring became the director of news for NBC
Radio.

Yet, despite this, Anita Miller, presiding over the California Commission on the status
of Women, charged the broadcast industry with tokenism: 'We've got to have more than
Barbara Walters. . . . We do not feel that when a single woman is promoted to co-anchor
person of a news program that it qualifies as an overall effort to really address the problem.'
Walters herself told the Survey:

> 'I don't see the day we'll have a woman anchor alone. If Harry Reasoner were to leave,
> there would be no question about me doing it alone. They would bring in a man. At NBC
> they made the decision to rake off Jim Hart, but they made Tom Brokaw co-host. But
> [after I left] they made Tom Brokaw the host and put the woman [Jane Pauley] in a
> subsidiary position. . . . They will not accept a woman as the head of the program. I
> can't imagine two females doing the news, as Chancellor and Brinkley. Of course they
> allow a woman alone on Sundays, but that's throwaway time.'

Lynn Scherr in a *Time* magazine interview in March 1977 reinforced Walters's view.
'Think of the possibility of two women anchors on a network news broadcast,' she said,
'and you'll understand we're still in the Ice Age.'

The small percentage of women who achieve management status in the industry rarely
attain parity with men in authority or pay. One young woman, a multiple award winner in
the nation's top radio market who asked to remain anonymous, was promoted to management when her male predecessor resigned. She kept her street reporting assignment along
with her new responsibilities and was given a $20 a week raise for doing both jobs. (The
station saved over $18,000 a year on the deal.) 'I would have advanced farther economically,'
she said, 'had I been a man. Because I am young and female my compensation for being

---

[7] Walters did not take over her spot until October 1976; Scherr began her public broadcasting job the
summer before.

the head of a department is abysmally low. A lot of blood is squeezed out of the female turnips at this station.' The summer of 1977 was a busy one for a reporter–producer, she said, referring to the metropolitan area blackout and the Son of Sam murders. She was told, nevertheless, that she would be paid for an 8-hr day only. (Her male predecessor had been paid overtime.) She accepts the dual resposibilities and long hours without fair compensation as 'a fact of life for most women who want to succeed in a man's world.'

Summing up the true status of women in the industry, Patricia Reed Scott, a former government press officer and now producer of the 1977 Emmy Award-winning series 'Getting On,' told the Survey:

'I was always aware that, excepting on-air reporters, hardly any women were visible in news assignment, line production, or any key policy positions. I still see too many women who work in broadcasting getting no further than production assistant, researcher, assistant-to, and producer of no-budget, ghetto-time public affairs.'

Perhaps one of the most scathing criticisms of the industry and the FCC came from the United Church of Christ in January 1977 in its annual report, 'Television Stations Employment Practices, 1976: the Status of Minorities and Women.' Although the UCC found a slight improvement for women in TV broadcasting, it remained skeptical. Dr. Ralph Jennings, associate director of the UCC's Office of Communications, in a report written with Alan T. Walters of Temple University, said he doubted his own job analysis. While overall employment of women in TV had risen since 1971, the year of the first study,[8] Jennings was concerned about the Federal Communications Commission reporting form (Form 395), which gave vague job titles subject to free interpretation, as well as manipulation by the licensees. Jennings said the job classifications 'do not fit the positions that exist in stations' and, as a result, 'can easily be distorted.' He claimed the FCC has 'ignored the need for tightening up its categories and has watered down its rules.' The report charged the industry with a continuing policy since 1971 of making 'paper promotions' to satisfy FCC equal employment opportunity requirements. Since 1971, according to the report, stations created 6122 upper-level jobs, while 3024 lower-level (clerical and service) posts have disappeared. Between 1975 and 1976 alone, upper-four jobs increased by 705 and lower-five jobs declined by 291 until today there are more than three upper-level employees in TV for every support member.

This increase in the number of higher-paying positions was also reported in the third annual FCC report released in the spring of 1977. According to the FCC, of 34,324 women employed full-time in 1976, 15,067 (or 44 per cent) held upper-four-category positions (or 17·7 per cent of these positions), an increase of 9·1 per cent over 1975.

'It seems improbable,' said Jennings, 'that this greatly increased corps of management personnel can function with reduced clerical support.' Jennings's boss, Dr. Everett C. Parker, director of the UCC, added that, while there are many honest broadcasters striving to raise the status of women and minorities, 'the fact that 78 per cent of all jobs are now reported to be in the upper level, higher-paying decision-making categories is proof that

---

[8] The report showed an increase from 19 per cent in 1971 to 42 per cent in 1976 for women in the upper four job categories (officials and managers, professionals, technicians, sales workers) while women in clerical posts dropped 22 per cent in this same period, from 77 per cent to 55 per cent of full-time women employees. (Clerical posts are in the lower five job categories, which also include craftsmen, operatives, laborers, and service workers.)

others are making paper promotions, taking advantage of FCC indifference to make
industry employment practices look better than they are.'

The murkiness of Form 395 made such deception easy.[9]

Reflecting this view, Professor John Abel and Judith Saxton of Michigan State University,
as a result of their own study of Form 395, filed a petition for rule making at the FCC with
a proposal for standardized industry-related employment categories. They contended,
'Women do not hold executive level positions in the broadcasting industry. They are
excluded from the decision-making process and, therefore, have no real influence on station
policy.'

In their brief to the FCC, Abel and Saxton said that the broadcast industry is a powerful
image creator and, thus, an important socializing force:

> 'It can be assumed that whoever occupies the executive level position at television stations
> across the country wields great power in influencing this socialization process. If a
> majority of these positions are held by only one segment of society, the ideas presented
> on television will reflect only the ideas of that one segment. If women are excluded from
> these positions, the picture being presented will be male oriented.'

Abel and Saxton were reiterating the concerns of women and minority advocates and
broadcast reformers. Any trend showing gains for women in broadcasting became suspect
as early as 1970 when the FCC adopted Form 395. A holdover required by the Equal
Employment Opportunity Commission of all federal contractors, the FCC admitted in its
report and order requiring the annual report, 'The appropriate job categories present a
difficult problem . . . are generalized and not particularly suited to the broadcast industry,'

Nevertheless, the commission adopted the form, justifying its use on the grounds that
'it would allow inter-industry comparisons and would simplify the reporting for all stations.'

At an NBC-owned and -operated station, a producer charged:

> 'The 395 Form that each station must file with the FCC giving EEO information lists
> many more women in the "Officials and Managers" category than can be found actually
> operating on that level. Many "Supervisors" and "Administrators" who are women are
> included in that category, no doubt.'

A news reporter in Houston said:

> '. . . As I understand it, one woman now categorized as office manager was before the
> EEO reports just a secretary, and the traffic director was also considered simply a clerk.
> We also have one woman who doubles as a receptionist-secretary and a reporter. I
> would not be surprised to see her listed under "professional" rather than "clerical." '

A reporter in Oklahoma City said:

> 'Being a producer (at this station), while it certainly is good for overall experience, is
> close to being a secretary. The title producer sounds big, but it involves no decisions

---

[9] The U.S. Civil Rights Commission study also condemns Form 395: 'The FCC Form 395 allows licensees
to imply erroneously that women and minorities are moving into decision-making positions when their
job titles and salaries suggest that they perform primarily clerical and routine administrative tasks.' In April
1977 the House of Representatives Subcommittee on Communications called for a review of Form 395 in its
Report of Findings and Recommendations of the Enforcement of Equal Opportunity and Antidiscrimination
Laws in Public Broadcasting.

regarding news format. . . . The producer more or less retypes scripts . . . types up run-downs, picks up slides for news stories.'

A reporter in St. Louis charged: 'I was given a phony title when hired, Director of Community Involvement Programs. . . . I was directing no one, not even myself.'

Yet, under chairperson Richard Wiley, the FCC refused to change its monitoring form. Further, the commission announced in mid-1976 a rule change which would eliminate some 6000 stations from the monitoring process despite the April 1977 House Subcommittee on Communications recommendations to the contrary. The agency proposed that only those stations with more than 10 employees be required to file an EEO report. It also exempted from filing a job title analysis (vital because Form 395 was not descriptive of the industry's jobs) those stations with less than 50 full-time employees. This new ruling would have exempted 88 per cent of the noncommercial TV and 100 per cent of the noncommercial radio stations. Richard Wiley defended the ruling as still covering 85 per cent of broadcast employees, or 92,000 jobs, and said it would provide for more realistic monitoring by reducing paperwork. Wiley also promised that the commission would utilize the time, energy, and resources saved in doing more on-site investigations. Jennings responded by calling the FCC 'the handmaiden of the industry it regulates,' and charged that, by exempting some two-thirds of the industry from filing, the FCC would be closing job entry and training doors for women and minorities.

However, in August 1977, in response to citizen groups, [10] the U.S. Court of Appeals for the Second Circuit, New York, unanimously struck down the new rules as 'arbitrary and capricious' and ordered the commission to return to its former practice. The appeals court ruling represented the first major victory for citizen groups since 1971, when the FCC adopted rules prohibiting broadcasters from discriminating in employment because of sex.

To date no license has been revoked on sex discrimination grounds. Moreover, by April 1977 only five hearings on EEO grounds had been held by the FCC.[11] This contradicts a promise made by Commissioner Wiley in August 1975 in an address to the Community Film Workshop Council in New York: 'Where it appears that the broadcaster has followed discriminatory employment practices, I can assure you that the commission will not hesitate to order a hearing to resolve any substantial and material questions of fact.'

Despite such protestations, a study by Citizens Communication Center (a public interest law firm in Washington, D.C.) showed substantial gaps in FCC enforcement of its EEO policies and charged that the FCC standards fall short of those applied by the courts in judging discrimination in employment. The Citizens Communication Center condemned the commission for allowing a licensee to upgrade its employment following a license challenge

---

[10] UCC, National Urban League, National Association for the Advancement of Colored People, Communications Commission of the National Council of Churches of Christ, and UNDA-USA (the national Catholic communications association).

[11] In April 1977, however, the U.S. Court of Appeals for the District of Columbia reversed the FCC license renewals of three broadcast stations without an FCC hearing; this decision would indicate that from now on the FCC will be required to stage more hearings on EEO issues.

and, thus, avoid a renewal hearing.[12] This particular practice was a major sore point in the U.S. Civil Rights Commission report, which read that the FCC

'Is not interested in eliminating discrimination by its licensees. Instead, it is interested only in learning that licensees intend to make "good faith effort" to provide equal employment opportunity.'

The commercial broadcast industry was not the only recalcitrant employer. The primary EEO battleground this year was waged in public broadcasting.

In April 1977 the Congress threatened to withhold federal funds unless public broadcasters came up with some hard facts, figures, and recommendations to implement findings of the 1975 Report of the Task Force on Women in Public Broadcasting.[13] The report charged 'pervasive under-representation of women in employment,' citing the fact that white males held 97 per cent and 98 per cent of the two top management positions in public TV stations (general manager and station manager).[14]

Furthermore, data submitted by the Corporation for Public Broadcasting in April 1977 to the Senate Appropriations Committee's Subcommittee on Labor, Health, Education and Welfare [15] showed an actual decline of 1 per cent in the proportion of women in the upper management levels in public television between January 1, 1976, and January 1, 1977.

Middle-management women in public broadcasting complained to the Survey of job titles with no authority or responsibility, and a reluctance on the part of management to promote qualified women. Two of the women who have since left public broadcasting said:

'All decision-making positions are filled by men. The only exception is executive producer and production teams for women's programs where the teams report to two male program executives. Virtually all assignments relating to the station's image are male.'

And: 'Management in public TV is white and male almost exclusively. . . . Departments often reject qualified women candidates who are brought to their attention.'

The DuPont correspondent in Memphis said: 'Public TV here is so short on women in key positions, they list the station manager's secretary on the masthead of the monthly program guide to add another female name.'

---

[12] This practice was notable in the case of WRC-TV Washington, D.C., in May 1972 when, over the opposition of NOW and the CCC, the FCC accepted updated employment statistics. Four years later, in February 1976, the FCC rejected EEOC's finding of discrimination and ruled WRC-TV's employment practices satisfied the public interest standards. Benjamin Hooks, then FCC EEO commissioner, while voting with the commission for renewal of the WRC-TV license, nevertheless questioned the process which denied a hearing and said, 'The commission must do more than summarily dismiss a petition to deny.' In April 1977 the U.S. Court of Appeals affirmed the FCC's renewal of the license and said the FCC may consider post-license term employment data in determining whether or not a broadcaster has complied with the EEOC's standards.

[13] The task force was established in November 1974 with the blessings of the CPB; the report was published and unanimously accepted by the CPB board in 1975.

[14] The UCC annual report in January 1977, analyzing FCC Form 395 employment figures, found that 80 per cent of upper-four-category jobs in public television (officials and managers, professionals, and technicians) are held by men at the 143 stations monitored.

[15] An EEO update required quarterly by a Senate report attached to public broadcasting's 1977 appropriations bill passed in 1976.

Lionel Van Deerlin (D-Cal.), chairperson of the House Subcommittee on Communications, in the Oversight Report on EEO Compliance condemned the Public Broadcasting Service's lack of improvement as 'bordering on negligence' and said 'CPB's continuing reluctance to impose tougher restrictions on its community service grants appears to stem as much from a fear of political reprisal by the stations as from a commitment to preserve its insulation from government interference.'

His statement reiterated earlier congressional threats. Representative Louis Stokes (D-Ohio), member of the Labor/HEW Appropriations Committee, had warned eight months earlier that, unless action is taken, 'Congress will be in the untenable position of unconstitutionally providing financial assistance to aid prohibited discriminatory conduct.' And, in February 1977, when Henry Loomis, president of the Corporation for Public Broadcasting, applied to Congress for an increase in funds for 1980, Senator Edward Brooke (R., Mass.) insisted that CPB show improvement in its female and minority record before he could comfortably approve new appropriations, and said he hoped employment problems could be solved without 'tacking an amendment on the appropriations bill.'

The major roadblock clearly centered around enforcement.

At the House Subcommittee on Communications hearings in August 1976, Loomis agreed that, while CPB is subject to Title VI and VII of the Civil Rights Act of 1964 and Title IX of the Education Amendments of 1972, once federal funds leave the CPB they are no longer considered to be federal funds in order to insulate receiving stations from the federal government influence on programming. Further, according to Loomis, compliance can be enforced only when a court or competent government agency, not the CPB, determines a station is in violation. This enforcement circle includes a catchall of federal agencies, each with its own regulations and authority: Justice Department. FCC, Department of Health, Education and Welfare, and the Equal Employment Opportunity Commission.[16]

Two months before these hearings the FCC, despite its plenary enforcement authority, had announced the changing of its monitoring rules over the objection of the public broadcasters, and also refused to consider their recommendation that Form 395 be made more relevant to broadcasting. Both actions on the part of the FCC would clearly hamstring any good intentions the public broadcasters might have had. Further, at the August hearings, FCC Chairman Wiley actually chided the public broadcasters for their EEO record and charged them with having a higher duty in this regard than do commercial broadcasters, since they operate partially on federal funds.

EEO enforcement in public broadcasting was a 'Catch 22' situation, prompting the Citizens Communication Center to ask, 'Where does the buck stop?' Every agency was caught in the enforcement bureaucracy, but each clung to its own territorial confines.

Thus, in April 1977, when the House subcommittee's report showed that Congress, too, was confused on enforcement, an inter-agency task force to include *all* the agencies was established to look into the problem. Chairperson Van Deerlin's committee report stated:

'[Admitting that] existing antidiscrimination laws appear to apply to stations, there are significant gaps in enforcement authority to render their application more apparent than real. . . . as a result of gaps in the law, inadequate personnel, and an overall lack of

---

[16] The FCC, due to the confining of EEOC jurisdiction to those employers with fifteen employees or over, is the only federal agency with plenary authority.

commitment, the federal agencies which share responsibility are doing a poor job of enforcement. There is little or no co-ordination of effort on the federal level.' [17]

Particularly called to task was the FCC: 'Unfortunately, the record of the FCC on EEO matters has been singularly disappointing. . . . The commission has shown an obvious reluctance to assert itself in handling EEO complaints.'

The report recommended to the FCC short-term license renewals for those stations not in compliance with EEO, a revision of the much criticized Form 395, an increase in the FCC's EEO personnel (presently there are just six people monitoring the employment records of 9224 TV and radio stations), and the development of a formal working arrangement with the EEOC to facilitate the exchange of information.

Enforcement proceedings were delayed for a few more months while still another committee looked into the matter. But the public broadcasters got their money and no amendment was attached to their appropriation.

In October 1977 President Jimmy Carter proposed a $1 billion package to aid the public broadcasters, this time with presidential strings attached. 'The Corporation, its grantees, subgrantees, contractors, and subcontractors shall be subject to the requirements of Title VI of the Civil Rights Act of 1964 and Title IX of the Education Amendments of 1972.' [18] Barry Jagoda, assistant to President Carter for media and public affairs, told the Survey:

'The bill makes it clear for the first time that the employment discrimination laws apply to stations and other producers that receive federal funds. . . . CPB will be under intense congressional scrutiny in this area.'

Frank Lloyd, White House Office of Telecommunications Policy, and one of the drafters of the bill, said:

'It now spells out that any recipients of funds are now subject to Titles VI and IX. This has never been clear before. It is the first time any President has addressed the issue as it applies to women in public broadcasting.'

While it is true that no president has addressed this particular issue with regard to women before, public broadcasting *has* been under intense congressional scrutiny in this area for over four years. Both the Justice Department and the Congress have held that public broadcasting is subject to Titles VI and IX.

Neither the House nor the Senate was pleased with the entire bill. Carolyn Sachs, staff assistant to Van Deerlin, said:

'Someone is going to have to bite the bullet. We were hoping to get the White House view [on the enforcement agency]. They did not make the hard decisions. It's a political involvement, trying to please too many people. The bill is too weak. By applying the provisions of Titles VI and IX to the CPB grants, the bill really does nothing more than confirm the findings of the subcommittee and sheds no additional light as to where EEO responsibility for enforcement lies.'

---

[17] House Subcommittee on Communications of the Committee on Interstate and Foreign Commerce, 'Report of Findings and Recommendations of the Enforcement of Equal Opportunity and Antidiscrimination Laws in Public Broadcasting,' April 1977.
[18] Public Broadcasting Financing Act of 1978.

As for the FCC being the agency of enforcement:

'Their record is not good and there must be some attention paid to clarifying their EEO response before we simply reaffirm their responsibility to public broadcasting EEO. The bottom line is there will be no further authorization until this is cleared up.'

The concern now is over a possible challenge to enforcement recommendations and even to the President's bill as it concerns them.[19] Lawyers differ on the interpretation of Titles VI and IX as they apply to public broadcasting. Originally the purpose of insulating public stations from government interference was to protect their rights on programming. Now it has become a political issue with the Congress, advocacy groups, and the White House on one side and the public broadcasting stations, fearful of infringement of their 'First Amendment' rights, on the other.

There are other important decisions to be made within the next year which may affect equal employment opportunity.

Two bills now before the Congress would give reimbursement to citizen groups to provide financial assistance for participation in agency proceedings.[20] FCC Commissioner Joseph Fogarty endorses financing (as did former commissioner Benjamin Hooks). Former FCC chief Wiley maintained that the leadership in public financing must come from the Congress and he did not, therefore, support any FCC rule making in favor of it.

The broadcasting industry is opposed to such financing. *Broadcasting* magazine, in an editorial in August 1977, charged that such funding 'would only enlarge the body of lawyers now mostly funded by foundations and specializing in attacking regulated businesses. . . . Public interest lawyers would begin recruiting litigants and magnifying or inventing grievances.'

This charge came on the heels of the Senate Government Affairs Committee report made earlier in the month which endorsed financing on the grounds that the public interest groups have a very small voice in agency proceedings while the regulated industries dominate. The report also said that public interest groups are hampered in proceedings because of lack of money. The report particularly singled out the poor record of the FCC in citizen participation proceedings.

In October 1977 FCC Commissioner Margita White said she expects a notice of proposed rule-making soon calling for revision of the much maligned Form 395. Support by fellow commissioner Fogarty, the new chairperson Charles Ferris, and the recently appointed commissioner Tyrone Brown is expected.

The public broadcasters announced in October 1977 a $190,000 commitment to help improve their job picture. People and Careers in Telecommunications is a nationwide job-matching system for women and minorities. Administered by the National Association of Educational Broadcasters, PACT will operate a job bank and placement service. Joseph Schubert, acting director of PACT, said, 'We are ready to become the headhunters for the industry.'

Thus, proposed legislation for financing indigent advocacy groups; new faces at the FCC; the return to the old FCC monitoring rules and the more than likely revision of Form 395; the congressional muscle that has brought some resolutions from the public broadcasters;

---

[19] In mid-October Frank Lloyd told Congress that the administration plans to submit an amendment in January 1978 providing for an EEO enforcement mechanism.

[20] The Kennedy-Mathias bill (S. 270) and H.R. 3361, introduced by Rep. Peter Rodino (D-N.J.)

the study of public broadcasting by the Carnegie Commission; the rewrite of the 1934 Communications Act; and the new Carter bill for public broadcasting, with the promise of an amendment for enforcement, could all bode well for women.

Nevertheless, present signs—such as consideration by the FCC of long-term license renewals for the industry as a whole and the reluctance of the FCC to hold hearings on challenged licenses—could offset any future gains for women in broadcasting. An immediate step by the Congress in the form of a realistic financial appropriation to the understaffed FCC EEO unit, along with legislation granting authority to the commission to levy fines on those stations not in compliance (monies to be used for training grants for women and minorities) would do much to further the cause.

Women are emerging from journalism schools in ever-increasing numbers. This year the graduate division of the Department of Journalism and Mass Communications at New York University enrolled forty-one men and eighty-three women. Professor David Rubin, chairperson of the department, commenting on the preponderance of women, said, 'We have no quotas. It is simply a matter of accepting the best people, and two-thirds of the best people in this class happen to be women.'

The enrollment of women at the Columbia Graduate School of Journalism rose from twenty-seven in a class of ninety in 1967 to seventy-nine in a class of 147 in 1977. Elie Abel, Dean of the school, said, 'The significant change is that women are now going after the management jobs, on the news desks, as editors, and in broadcasting as producers.'

Carolyn Wean, news director at KDKA-TV in Pittsburgh, told the Survey:

'The long-range test of how the changing role of women in society will affect the role of women in broadcasting is yet to be seen. The clues to any results will only be seen in the next five to ten years when and if the pool of women now in broadcasting share a larger portion of the middle and top level management positions.'

In the years to come it would be a sad commentary if women were to reiterate Professor Kenneth B. Clark's warning to the Kerner Commission on Civil Disorders in 1967: 'It is . . . a kind of Alice in Wonderland . . . with the same moving picture shown over and over again . . . and the same inaction.'

*In March 1979 the United States House of Representatives Communications Sub-committee introduced their second rewrite of the 1934 Communications Act. Among the sweeping changes is the total elimination of equal employment opportunity provisions for women through the deregulation of the entire industry—radio now and television in 10 years.

The new structure, relying totally on 'marketplace forces' to advance the public interest, would determine the course of the industry for years to come as well as the role and future of the women in it.

To satisfy public interest groups the rewrite provides for an office of consumer affairs as well as a provision permitting the reimbursement of citizen groups for participation in FCC rulemakings and committee proceedings.[21] However, the present form gives no

---

* This section is an update of the original article.
[21] The FCC provision is, perhaps, academic as the very future of the Commission is in doubt for the new rewrite would abolish it, replacing it with a similar body having no power over station performance.

incentive for male management to hire women in upper management positions and no protection to those women attempting the corporate climb. Given the record of the broadcasters, the rewrite to date offers no *cause célèbre*.

Moreover, in January 1979 the United States Commission on Civil Rights in an update of their 1977 report, 'Window Dressing on the Set: Women and Minorities in Television,' reported to President Jimmy Carter that in the period since their initial study women have made no significant progress. White males continue to hold the vast majority of official and management positions.

And in public broadcasting, the long-awaited Carnegie Commission Report published in April 1979 found that women and minorities have indeed been the 'target of discrimination.' The Commission called for their placement in leadership positions on all public broadcasting governing boards as well as for the immediate implementation of professional training and career development programs.

The prestigious Radio Television News Directors Association, in yet another study, released its latest findings in the January 1979 issue of its trade publication, *Communicator*. Ironically, while the survey boasted gains for women in radio and television newsrooms, not one of its 29 board members listed in the same edition is a woman. Every officer, all regional directors, and directors at large are men!

In April 1979 the FCC's seventh annual report on employment practices showed 52 per cent of all women employees in broadcasting were in the top jobs, an actual 4 per cent increase since 1977. Again, any gains must be suspect as the FCC has not yet revised its 395 job reporting form, and an inaccurate picture of the job status of women continues with titles artificially inflated. After an earlier notice of rule-making, the FCC in 1978 did finally approve a modified version of the form with an additional requirement for licensees to rank employees according to salary and to identify women and minorities. The latter generated so much criticism by the National Association of Broadcasters that the FCC delayed revision once again.

But, while the current status of 395 is disappointing, the FCC and the Equal Employment Opportunity Commission have established closer co-ordination through a memorandum of understanding in which they agreed to exchange information about a broadcaster's employment practices and to set forth each agency's responsibilities for handling complaints about employment discrimination.

So, while NBC appointed a woman, Jane Cahill Pfeiffer, to be its new chairperson and President Carter appointed another woman, Anne Jones, to succeed Margita White at the FCC, Barbara Walters did not—as she predicted—become sole anchor when her male counterpart, Harry Reasoner, left ABC in 1978. Walters found herself instead reduced to one quarter of her original self on a team which now includes three others—all men.

In 1977 ABC's Lynn Scherr said that women are still in the Ice Age. In 1979 we see no chance of a thaw.

Women's Studies Int. Quart., 1980, Vol. 3, pp. 15–27
Pergamon Press Ltd.   Printed in Great Britain

WATCHING THE FAMILY*

JANE BOOTH

23 Carden Road, Peckham, London, S.E.15, U.K.

(Accepted August 1979)

Synopsis—*The Pattern of Marriage* was a four-part television documentary produced by the BBC in 1953. It followed a young couple through courtship to marriage, the birth of their first child, marital problems which lead to a temporary separation, and their final reconciliation. It was based on the notion of the family as the basic unit of social organization, and it attempted to construct its family audience as a secure unit which, although not without its internal difficulties, must be upheld.

This paper sets out to show how the BBC felt a duty to re-establish the 'happy family' as a norm and how this was implemented through specific BBC policy. It examines the BBC's definition of an 'ordinary' family and the audience response to that constructed definition. It also looks at how the BBC, in relation to its understanding of the post-war period, 'dealt with' the image of the family and the 'pattern of marriage' on television in the early 1950s.

INTRODUCTION

The Pattern of Marriage was a four-part television documentary produced in 1953 at a time when the British Broadcasting Corporation regarded the increasing number of broken marriages since the war as a worrying problem. It followed a young couple through courtship to marriage, the birth of their first child, marital difficulties which lead to a temporary separation, and their final reconciliation.

Caryl Doncaster, the producer, director and co-writer used drama documentary techniques to achieve as realistic a portrayal as possible. As a 'documentary', the series carried with it certain assumptions of truth and reality and was considered progressive in its day. The combination of familiar, emotive subject-matter and 'realistic' portrayal provoked much comment from both the public and media professionals.

The Pattern of Marriage was based on the notion of the family as the basic unit of social organization and it attempted to reconstruct its family audience through its representation of the family as a secure unit which, although not without its internal difficulties, must be upheld.

This paper sets out to show how the BBC felt its duty was to re-establish the 'happy family' as a norm and how this was implemented through specific BBC policy. It examines the BBC's definition of an 'ordinary' family at the time and the audience response to that constructed definition. It also looks at how the BBC, in relation to its understanding of the post-war period, 'dealt with' the image of the family and the 'pattern of marriage' in the early 1950s.

With the advent of radio broadcasting, the BBC was genuinely concerned about its effects on the family—whether it would restrict the public's ability or desire to socialize, entertain, continue with hobbies, even to talk to each other. A survey on radio's social effects was conducted by the BBC in 1939:

---

* My thanks to Paddy Scannell for help and advice and to Helen Baehr for editorial assistance.

'Formerly the mutual interests and experience of the various members of the family were very limited. The doings, illnesses of neighbours, weddings, births and funerals in the street formed the main topics common to all. Broadcasting has supplied, not only a new way of spending leisure time by family "listening in", but a vastly wider range of conversation: "In the old days, one would start chipping in, and then another and it would end in a quarrel. Now they all sit listening to the wireless instead of quarrelling." '[1]

The BBC saw its audience, then, as individuals grouped in families, and it was this assumption of the family as a secure, stable environment in which one could lead a happy and fulfilled life, that affected policy decisions in the early days of broadcasting.

'The place of listener research within the BBC can only be freed from all ambiguity by stating unequivocally that even if it revealed that a majority of the public were opposed to a policy which was being pursued by the BBC, that itself would not be considered a valid reason why the policy should be reversed, or the programmes withdrawn. This would not be to say that the listener research findings would be ignored; they would be considered with the utmost care and weighed with other considerations which were relevant. But the decision when taken would be a responsible one to come in the light of what was considered ultimately to be in the best interest of the public and public service' (report from the Broadcasting Committee, 1949).[2]

Up until the appearance of *The Pattern of Marriage* on television in 1953 there had been, on radio, a number of cosy middle-class family serials—*The English Family Robinson*, *Life with the Lyons*, and *The Dales*, to name a few. They all, by assertions of typicality and 'ordinariness', assumed every family was middle class, basically non-problematic and essentially happy. David Nathan comments on radio's portrayal of the family at the time:

'The sacred family, the backbone of situation comedy, in which the scatter-brained wife and good-hearted hubby faced life's little middle class upheavals with a barrage of quick fire quips . . . but then appeared . . . the atrocious Glums.'[3]

The Glums were a working-class family who appeared to challenge this standard representation. They began as a regular spot on Dennis Norden and Frank Muir's *Take It From Here*, and had gained considerable popularity by the early 1950s. Norden:

'What we did was send up relationships between people, family relationships, things that were sacrosanct at the time, Ron and Eth started from a sketch we did about an engaged couple. There were a lot of cosy family serials and soap operas on the radio, so it was a slight send up of them too.'[4]

It was this reaction against the mainstream of media output which in the mid 1960s created *Till Death Us Do Part*. Johnny Speight:

'I didn't create Alf Garnett, society created him. All I did was report him.'[5]

---

[1] Jennings, Hilda and Gill, Winifred, on behalf of the BBC. July 1939. *Broadcasting in Everyday Life*, a survey of the social effects of television, p. 23. BBC, London.
[2] *Report of the Broadcasting Committee*. September 1949. Volume 11, p. 143, London, BBC.
[3] Nathan, David. 1971. *The Laughtermakers: a Quest for Comedy*, p. 19. Peter Owen, London.
[4] Norden, Dennis, quoted in *ibid*, p. 30.
[5] Speight, Johnny, quoted in *op. cit.* note 3, p. 30.

It can be argued, though, that this 'alternative' view of the family served as much to re-enforce as to criticize the conventional, accepted definitions, remaining as they did within the strict confines of comedy.

The media offer an interpretation of the family which is legitimated through the 'consensus model'—where society is assumed to be composed of individuals who share agreed, taken-for-granted, commonsense definitions of reality. The Royal Family are living, legitimating examples of this model:

'. . . a highly visible embodiment of national identity. Broadcasting gave the crown a quite new and contemporary *presence* in national life.'[6]

The Queen's annual speech at Christmas, traditionally a family time and Richard Cawston's documentary, show the Royal Family without regal paraphernalia, looking almost 'ordinary'. The family transcends all class boundaries if it unites both the Queen and 'Joan Public' as 'mothers' with 'husbands' and 'children'.

James Halloran:

'The media's function is the provision of social realities where they did not exist before, or the giving of new directions to tendencies already present, in such a way that the adoption of the new attitude or form of behaviour is made a socially acceptable mode of conduct, whilst failure to adopt is represented as socially disapproved deviance.'[7]

The mass media provide us with a picture of social reality which we can do very little about' other than accept: a reality of facts, norms, values and experiences.

Documentary's claim is to complete social reality, presenting itself as a mirror on the world, reflecting an unmediated image. Grierson: 'The job of documentary is to explain society to society.' It claims to re-present reality by re-capturing or re-creating spontaneous, and therefore authentic, actuality. Its goal is the quest for truth, the equipment is used, it appears, merely for information-gathering purposes. Subjects speak for themselves (when they are provided with the technology), in their own surroundings, about their own experiences. They lack the professionalism of the experienced media personality and therefore appear unmediated and more 'real'.

Before light, inexpensive, conveniently transportable camera equipment was available, reality had to be re-created in the studio, with actors and actresses.

'The form of drama documentary was a practical solution to the limited options available within a television service lacking any full-scale facilities for documentary film work.'[8]

In 1953, Caryl Doncaster was restricted to only a few filmed inserts. The rest had to be studio-based and go out 'live'.

'The form developed as an adaptation to these circumstances, seeking to disguise as far as possible the obstacles and limitations implicit in any studio based reconstruction of social reality from the world outside.'[9]

Research was carried out during months of close contact with the subject itself. Duncan Ross:

---

[6] Scannell, G. P. 1979. *The Realities of Television, 1946–1955, Media, Culture and Society* **1** (1), 4.
[7] Halloran, James. 1970. *The Effects of Television*, p. 29. Panther, London.
[8] Scannell, G. P. *op. cit.* note 6, p. 6.
[9] *Ibid.*

'There can be no worthwhile documentary until there has been "intercourse with the thing itself and it has been lived with." ' [10]

For *The Pattern of Marriage*, Caryl Doncaster began her research at the beginning of October, 1952, which continued until the programmes were finally transmitted between March 11th and May 22nd, 1953.

Drama documentary's influences ranged from the radio feature, the documentary film movement, to television talks of the time, and itself later proved to be an influence on the increasingly popular film documentary: it defined a research method and orientation towards the subject, which, combined with its obvious sense of realism, influenced future documentaries and, indeed, television drama.[11]

THE PATTERN OF MARRIAGE

Before working on *The Pattern of Marriage*, Caryl Doncaster directed *The Rising Twenties*, a television series illustrating the different problems and outlooks of teenagers in Britain. In all her work she used the drama documentary technique in an attempt to highlight current social problems.

The war had a tremendous influence on the family unit and no institution was more aware of the problems of readjustment than the BBC. To help with the difficulties of coming to terms with post-war life, the BBC broadcast twelve programmes under the title *Family Relationships* in 1946. Each programme began with a case study of a particular family and a discussion on its problems, asking questions such as—'Is the war responsible? How far must the family, its habits and ideas, change in a changing world?' In the same year another series appeared, *Happy Families*, in which 'typical', usually middle-class, families were chosen to talk about themselves. Episode two featured the Browns and was described as 'a programme for the Browns and all about the Browns.' Later that year *Family Album* was broadcast: 'the true story of a professional middle-class family, where mother and father and eight children live the sort of family life which is rapidly disappearing as the old order changes' (*Radio Times*).

'1951 saw the end of wartime dislocations in family life, and the beginning of what we must regard as normality.' [12]

After the post-war peak, marriages in the early fifties were being dissolved at the rate of 30,000 per year—four times the level of immediate pre-war years. The Royal Commission on Marriage and Divorce, appointed in 1951 to enquire into the law of England and Scotland concerning divorce, declared in 1955 that divorce by consent would lead to disaster:

'It may become necessary to consider whether the community as a whole would not be happier and more stable if it abolished divorce altogether.' [13]

---

[10] Ross, Duncan. Spring 1950. The documentary in television. *BBC Q.* **5**.

[11] Scannell, G. P. *op. cit.*, note 6, p. 6.

[12] Mr. Brayshaw, A. J. General Secretary of the National Marriage Guidance Council (herewith referred to as Gen. Sec. NMGC), in a letter to Caryl Doncaster, February 24, 1953. This document can be located in the BBC Written Archive centre, Caversham Park, Reading, for further reference. Herewith, all documents which can be located in the Archive Centre will be marked (BBC Arch.).

[13] Lewis, Peter. 1958. *The Fifties*. Heinemann, London, quoting on the Report on the Royal Commission on Marriage and Divorce, set up in 1951.

The Welfare State, introduced shortly after the Second World War, provided social services which were used as a bargaining force in the wage struggle, along with new safety regulations, pensions, health schemes and longer holidays.[14] In the 'affluent fifties', poverty was thought to be rapidly in decline.

'This myth was welcomed by both the Tories and Labour, the Tories because it meant that Tory freedom worked, the Labour Party because it meant that the Welfare State worked.'[15]

This meant that the 'few' remaining poor were in some way to blame for their situation. The 'problem family' was born.

'A problem family is one that lives in squalor and is content to do so. It apparently suffers from domestic and possibly social ineducability' (report from the Eugenics Society, 1947).

In *The Pattern of Marriage*, Caryl Doncaster set out to portray on television the problems encountered by 'an ordinary family' in such a way that they appeared surmountable. The documentary was produced and directed by Caryl Doncaster and written in conjunction with Ted Willis. It follows a young couple, Peggy and David, through four particular stages in their life together—marriage, the problem of finding a house, the birth of their first child, and the potential breakdown of their marriage. The programmes were classed as 'documentaries' but were in fact 'drama documentaries'. Extensive research was carried out by both Caryl Doncaster and Ted Willis into all the issues dealt with in the series. A script was produced based upon this research and actors were chosen. Caryl Doncaster:

'We discovered Billy Whitelaw and David Byrne for the series—using them as unknowns so that people would get a feeling of reality.' (Caryl Doncaster; letter to the author, March 1979).

Studio sets were used for most of the series but some film was shot on location.

In episode one, *A Home of Their Own*, we are introduced to the characters and their social background. Peggy, aged twenty, is the only daughter of lower middle-class parents and David, twenty-six, lives in the same area with his widowed mother, described as working-class. He is a skilled craftsman, working in the same aircraft factory as Peggy. They are planning to marry, with parental consent. Wedding preparations begin and the couple attempt to find somewhere to live. They are eventually forced to accept a long standing offer from David's mother, Mrs. Mason, to share her ground floor flat. They would all three have to share the kitchen and would share the bathroom with the family upstairs.

Episode two, *Two's Company*, 'shows the corners being rubbed off during the first year of marriage' (Caryl Doncaster). We see Peggy working in the house while David relaxes. She visits the doctor accompanied by her close friend Kathie. This episode was anticipated by Caryl Doncaster and her peers to be the most controversial of the four, with its references, however vague, to sex and contraception. We establish that Peggy is pregnant.

Episode three, *A Son*, begins in hospital. As soon as Peggy arrives home with the baby, David begins studying for qualifications to try for a better job. Peggy feels cut off from the outside world, left at home with the baby. Mrs. Mason solves their accomodation problem

[14] Wilson, Elizabeth. 1977. *Women and the Welfare State*. Tavistock, London.
[15] *Ibid.*

by moving upstairs but other problems occur. David, bored with homelife, begins to take out Blanche, a girl from work.

A crisis is reached in episode four, *For Better, For Worse*, when Peggy finds out about Blanche and returns to her parents home with the baby, resolving to divorce David. She visits the Probation Officer for advice who invites her to court to witness other separation cases. David also arrives to see the Probation Officer, sent by Kathie. The couple are reconciled. Episode four ends with the wedding of another couple, symbolizing Peggy and David's reunion.

BBC POLICY

Doncaster originally described the series as:

'a realistic look at what leads a married couple into the divorce courts . . . the way of tackling the issues involved might well be to take one reasonable couple and follow them through courtship to marriage breakdown.' [16]

She saw her role of documentary-maker as one closely connected with the BBC's Reithian policy of public service:

'Married life and the home being the core of our society, a BBC TV programme series which sets out to show the family in the home and the problems arising from marriage would be of service to such homes.' [17]

Throughout the BBC, from its policy-making committees to its assumptions of the viewing public, lies the notion of the family as the primary structural unit of society, and the 'happy family' at that. It is the institutional and social norm by which the boundaries of good taste, sense and decorum are gauged. So, a series such as *The Pattern of Marriage* which portrays anything but a happy family, and indeed makes the problems of marriage its focal point, policy-wise is bound to run into difficulties. Conflict arises between the need to recognize the family as a problem and at the same time rescue and re-establish it as the ideal unit of social organization.

Problems encountered by our adopted television family include the difficulties in finding suitable accomodation, the problems involved in child-bearing and consequent unhappy domestic relations and sex (dealt with rather non-specifically), which all lead to the threat of complete marital breakdown culminating in divorce, or the search through institutions such as the National Marriage Guidance Council (NMGC), for some kind of marriage rescue operation. The ending inevitably leads to the re-instatement of Peggy and David firmly within their happy home, complete with baby, their marriage once again intact and ready to start on their second round of 'happy families'.

Caryl Doncaster also recognized this conflict which she resolved by describing the series almost as if it was a guide for marriage—aspects of marriage and family life to watch out for and avoid. This role of the programme was re-enforced by the General Secretary of the NMGC:

'Besides being good entertainment and true to life, your scripts make a really valuable contribution to family life and I am certain that any young couples seeing them will,

---

[16] Doncaster, Caryl, to Cecil McGivern, Controller of Programmes, October 14, 1952 (BBC Arch.).
[17] *ibid.*

in consequence, give more thought and effort to the success of their marriages. Everyone deplores the large number of broken marriages. Everyone says rather vaguely that it should be prevented by education. The real difficulty is to find the means of such education and I think your programmes are a major contribution to this end . . . . I request that the programmes should be filmed and made available, if possible, for Marriage Guidance Councils to use all over the country.' [18]

In the course of her research, she talked to doctors, priests, marriage guidance officials, probation officers and lawyers—all authoritative and legitimating sources, professionally qualified to define the problems. Along with Ted Willis, she met newly-married couples, mothers in maternity hospitals, and sat for days in divorce and magistrate's courts. Caryl Doncaster:

'We soon realized that the field was too enormous, the material too various to deal with in cross section. So we focused our story on one couple. Two ordinary young people working in the same factory fall in love, become engaged and decide to get married. It's the old story set against today's social background. We hope that watching the struggles of this particular young couple during the early years of their married life will throw some light on the problems and special difficulties that all young people have to face when setting up home nowadays.' [19]

So why were Peggy and David chosen and who dictated what their fate should be? The script writer has a choice—either the issues which s/he considers important determine what happens to the characters or the characters themselves determine the number of issues raised. By describing Peggy and David as an ordinary couple, Caryl Doncaster had already reduced the number of issues it was possible to raise concerning them. 'Ordinary' meant the BBC's conception of 'ordinary' which in turn meant the BBC's conception of its audience—the 'ordinary' family. Once the couple's typicality had been established, rules and conventions came into play regarding audience expectations and compliance with BBC policy.

From the viewers' research reports compiled after each episode, it seems that these conventions were generally adhered to. Retired salesman:

'It was so pleasant to meet a really down to earth family, and a change from the sugar and spice of the cinema.'

Woman:

'We enjoyed the programme because it brought back the time immediately following our marriage, 30 years ago.'

Issues raised in the course of the series which caused general ideological and policy problems for the BBC were marriage, sex (within the boundaries of marriage only), religion and divorce. Looking back on the series, Caryl Doncaster:

'As far as I can remember, I had no social restrictions other than the taste of the time as reflected in my production and Mr. Willis' writing. The only lines we had to alter slightly were to do with birth control' (from letter to author, March 1979).

---

[18] Gen. Sec. NMGC in a letter to Caryl Doncaster, March 21 1953.
[19] Doncaster, Caryl, in an article submitted to the *Radio Times* to introduce the series, *The Pattern of Marriage*, March 2, 1953 (BBC Arch.).

If she did not have to alter any of the script, it was because the restrictions were imposed long before she began to write it.

The general viewer is addressed as a responsible citizen, with taste and a sense of morality and decency which at all costs should not be offended. S/he is part of a chain which links together the family, other responsible citizens, home, leisure, work, community and the nation.

BBC policy is grounded in this notion of unifying the many diverse elements in society by treating them in the same neutral, non-political way. The issues raised in *The Pattern of Marriage* were therefore bound to pose problems in the area of BBC policy.

BBC POLICY—SEX

Sex was the issue which, inevitably, caused the most controversy. Nest Bradney, publicity officer for the BBC:

'Of the four programmes, the one on which we expect reaction is number two, i.e. the programme about the physical side of marriage. It is for that reason that I have disposed of all four programmes in one write-up for *Television News* in the hope that number two will miss particular attention. The point to note is that programme two deals with the problem of adjustment in the first year of marriage and that sex is only one of the problems. The script allows the doctor to say that if she wants family planning, he is at her service, thus not involving people whose religion is otherwise.' [20]

On the question of sex, Caryl Doncaster consulted the NMGC, a representative of the Church of England and the Roman Catholic Advisory Council. At the time, they were the only authorities available both to comment on such matters, and who were also considered to be 'experts' by the BBC and the viewing public. They all agreed that sexual problems were partially to blame for most marriage breakdowns. Sexual problems, however, were restricted to the purely physical, isolated from the whole question of sex roles and sexual politics. A directive regarding BBC policy which was still unchallenged at that time, however, forbade any mention of 'the physical side of marriage' or of family planning. Caryl Doncaster:

'The physical element plays its part in all marriages, happy or otherwise, and I do not believe that we can leave it out completely. When we come to marriage breakdown, although authorities all differ as to the importance and relative position of the physical element, no authority states that it doesn't exist . . . if we leave this side out of the picture therefore, it is my opinion that we will not be fulfilling our obligation to viewers to put all the issues before them. If we include it, it is extremely difficult to put it in such a way in dramatized dialogue on a TV screen that would be valid or acceptable to the public.' [21]

So although within the context of the series, sex was one of the major issues, because of policy restrictions, it (and Peggy) remained virtually untouched.
David:

'Peggy, darling, I want you, I need you, I can't go on like this, having you so near, and yet so far . . .'

---

[20] Bradney, Nest, Publicity Officer to the BBC, in a letter to Caryl Doncaster, February 19, 1953 (BBC Arch.).
[21] Doncaster, Caryl, in a letter to Cecil McGivern, October 7, 1952 (BBC Arch.).

Peggy:

> 'Dave . . . if it's that, you've only got to ask me . . . I'll come away with you . . . we'll find some excuse this weekend. I love you David. I want you to be happy.'

David replies that of course they can, and should, wait. It is clear, though, that female sexuality is defined purely in male terms—'I want you to be happy'. Peggy's 'unselfish offer' is made to gratify David's needs. The subject is brought up again when Peggy, worried because she doesn't enjoy sex and not able to tell David, is persuaded by her friend (another woman) to see the doctor.

Doctor:

> 'It's simply lack of knowledge, Mrs. Mason . . . It's something for which you're not to blame and certainly you've no need to feel ashamed about it. Too many people think that love making, which after all is one of the most important foundations for a happy marriage, comes naturally. It's a technique, an art, and it has to be learned.'

The doctor serves as a reassuring figure to a nation of women pressurised by the media to experience sexual fulfilment and at the same time refused any real means of sexual liberation. In 1951, Eliot Slater and Moya Woodside discovered,

> 'By the fifties, sexual potency in men and sexual responsiveness in women began to be seen as explicitly desirable qualities.' [22]

This was emphasised through such institutions as magazine problem pages. Peggy's 'problem', then, was reduced to one simply of technique, something which *she* could overcome with practice. It is *she* who feels inadequate, who takes responsibility and looks for help, who sees *herself* as having 'failed'. The situation is not put into any wider context, it is not discussed either by the doctor or the couple themselves. The advice given is totally inadequate but, because the subject has been mentioned and commented upon by a recognized authority, it can be closed.

Audience reaction was favourable, according to the viewer surveys:

> 'The programme was warmly commended for breaking new ground in discussing with a frankness that was only occasionally considered indiscreet, the more intimate side of the family relationship.'

Leonard Mosely writes in the *Daily Express* (April 9, 1953):

> 'It was pretty frank, and I dare say somewhat startling to people who, "don't like to talk about these things". But it could surely have caused no embarrassment to reasonable people.'

BBC POLICY—RELIGION

Religion was another source of conflict and much discussion. Caryl Doncaster used the vicar as an authoritative father figure to legitimate and contextualize the position of marriage:

---

[22] Quoted by Wilson, Elizabeth, *op. cit.*, note 14.

Vicar:

> 'You may feel your marriage is a purely personal affair. But it is a bit more than that, you know. It affects other people in a great many ways, and that is why society is interested in your getting married. A wedding is just about the most important event in any community, it's a social act.' (Transcript from episode one, *A Home of Their Own*).

During her research, Caryl Doncaster found opinion varied wildly as to what should be said by the vicar to the young couple on the subject of sex—from the 'new wave' Rev. Reindorp:

> 'No parson who is within a mile of doing his job would dream of marrying a couple without going sufficiently into the whole question of sexual relationships.'

to the rather more conventional Rev. F. H. House, Head of Religious Broadcasting in the BBC:

> 'I have talked with two very active and well liked and respected parish priests working in parishes similar to that in which Peggy and David are presumed to be living, and on the basis of their practice I am quite certain that Reindorp is greatly exaggerating the number of parsons who do what he does.'

A constant check was kept upon every subject which may arouse concern or offend the sensibilities of the audience. Although the tolerance level of the audience was anticipated correctly, so as only to attract letters of congratulation, some of the daily papers, the popular press in particular, were not so receptive:
Daily Mirror (March 20, 1953) headline—'Marrying—Don't'.

> 'Of all the TV programmes we old codgers have seen since TV first started, this was the worst. Why did we watch it? Dammit, we couldn't turn it off. We were mesmerised by the piffle—the incredible hambone junk of the play. If this rubbish was passed by NMGC then the sooner the council is reformed, the better.'

This, however was a minority reaction expressed by *The Mirror*, and one not endorsed by any of the 'quality' papers.

The ending was obviously problematic—a series which claimed to 'throw some light on the problems and special difficulties that all young people have to face when setting up home nowadays' could hardly end in divorce if the BBC was to endorse the value and importance of the stability of marriage. From the audience research reports, the programme's charm seemed to lie in its accurate portrayal of the teething problems experienced by newly-weds. One woman's comment:

> 'It brought back the time immediately following our marriage, 30 years ago . . . . not much different to what we remember.'

The expectation was obviously that in 30 years, Peggy and David too would look back at their early days with the same kind of hazy nostalgia; that their problems were only teething problems, to be expected at the beginning of every marriage; that they do not represent a serious, continuing reality. Any confrontation of issues which might have occurred has been neatly avoided.

BBC POLICY—MARITAL BREAKDOWN

On the question of marital breakdown and divorce, Caryl Doncaster consulted trusted organizations such as the NMGC for BBC policy guidelines. She was issued with a directive:

'The BBC must not say anything about any aspect of marriage guidance which might impair the delicate balance kept on this subject.' [23]

She kept in close contact throughout the research period with Mr. A. J. Brayshaw, General Secretary of the NMGC. Mr. Brayshaw listed (a) having to live with in-laws, (b) selfishness in sexual and money matters, and (c) immaturity as the main causes of marital stress. There was no attempt made, however, within the context of the series, to locate these problems within a society in need of change.

Caryl Doncaster also contacted a representative from the Ministry of Health:

'The Ministry of Health feels as the series is being watched by so many people and is arousing so much interest in the press, it is more vital than ever to leave young couples at the end of the series with a more optimistic picture than that of Peggy and David going through the hands of the Probation Officer at the Magistrate's court. This could be done by putting into the mouth of the Probation Officer that this couple had been very unlucky in the combination of circumstances that led to their appearance in the court, and now that they were receiving help from all sides of society, they must now do their best to help themselves.' [24]

Always the assumption being that the couple will remain a couple, despite present problems. Although Peggy and David do not actually proceed with divorce, its existence need not totally be denied. Caryl Doncaster:

'Our central couple only get as far as the solicitor's office and a magistrate's court before a reconciliation, and any strong sectional views cutting across even this can be brought out by subsidiary characters. I do not think any useful purpose would be served by showing the divorce courts in action. We have decided, however, that all we need to show is a magistrate's court dealing with separation and maintenance cases, with the implication that among these cases there are some that must inevitably go further to the divorce courts.'

The issue is therefore 'dealt with' in BBC terms by suggestion and implication whilst still endorsing the position of the stable family unit in society and preserving that 'very difficult balance the BBC tries to keep' on the question of marriage and marriage breakdown. The subject is kept firmly within the boundaries of the social 'victims' (Peggy and David) and the social services. Thus the social precludes the political—it cannot be subject to political analysis as political issues at this time demanded a different treatment.

'The political subject is structured as an accomodation to the concerns of those in political authority; whereas the social subject is structured from *our* point of view (i.e. the audience), and our concerns with the current problem areas in our society.' [25]

---

[23] Doncaster, Caryl, notes made after meeting (BBC Arch.).
[24] Doncaster, Caryl, in a letter to Cecil McGivern, after an interview with a representative from the Ministry of Health, Dr. Dorothy Taylor, authority on Maternal and Child Welfare (BBC Arch.).
[25] Scannell, G. P. *op. cit.*, note 6.

CONCLUSION

The use of the documentary technique in television itself commands a certain authority and claims unspoken assumptions of truth and impartiality. Drama documentary commands the same attention whilst allowing the director a greater degree of freedom.

The Pattern of Marriage was based on the notion of the family as the basic unit of social organization. It attempted to reconstruct its assumed family audience through the drama documentary technique, and to anticipate problems which 'an average family might encounter'. [26] Caryl Doncaster was therefore able to stereotype characters as typical mothers, daughters, i.e. characters with definite roles within the family, and still make the claims of reality implicit within the documentary format.

During the fifties, the BBC had a paternal, protective attitude towards its audience, and regarded itself as an influential force in society. The strict controls on Caryl Doncaster, imposed from both inside and outside the BBC, indicate that the family was a subject of national concern, not just of internal policy wrangles. Audience reaction was anticipated to the finest nuance, and any issue which showed even a hint of provoking a negative response was rethought and couched in more 'acceptable' terms. Television offered an image of the family from which it was impossible to deviate.

The family was seen as a small secure unit, separate from the politics of 'outside', with allegiances primarily to itself—'blood is thicker than water', and 'look after your own' are its slogans. Anything which threatened the family was seen as a threat to the nation as a whole, the two were assumed to be definitely linked.

> 'We have a chain that starts with the 'ordinary' person and links together family, community and nation through relations between family and community, family and family, parents and children, person and work and family and home.' [27]

Marital conflicts are located firmly within the family unit itself. David's mother resolves the couple's housing problem, the *only* problem which was regarded as society's fault, and the couple are encouraged to solve their own personal conflicts:
Peggy:

> 'What's the answer? More housing, more nurseries?'

Ms. Castle (Probation Officer):

> 'All that would help. I think it's the duty of society to give its newly-weds a fair break; but the final answer rests with the people themselves' (transcript from episode four, *For Better, For Worse*).

The framework for the series was clearly set within the boundaries of family and family experience, and so transcended all class definitions—anyone could experience the same problems if they were part of a family. The series ends on a triumphant note with the couple's reconciliation. It is a 'happy ending', not only because they are reunited, but because the family structure has remained unchallenged, indeed it has been emphasized.

---

[26] Doncaster, Caryl. *op. cit.*, note 16.
[27] Birmingham Centre for Contemporary Cultural Studies, literature sub-group, *The Thirties—A Literary Decade?*

REFERENCES

Anderson, Michael. 1976. *Sociology of the Family*. Penguin Modern Sociology Readings.

Birmingham Centre for Contemporary Cultural Studies, literature sub-group, *The Thirties—A Literary Decade*.

Briggs, Asa. 1961, 1965, 1970. *The History of Broadcasting in the United Kingdom*, 3 Vols. Oxford University Press, Oxford.

Cooper, David, 1976. *The Death of the Family*. Pelican, Harmondsworth.

Curran, J., Gurevitch, M. and Woollacot, J., eds. 1977. *Mass Communication and Society*. Edward Arnold for the Open University.

Garnham, Nicholas. 1978. *Structures of Television*, BFI Television Monograph.

Halloran, James D. 1970. *The effects of Television*. Panther, London.

Heller, Caroline. 1978. *Broadcasting and Accountability*, BFI Television Monograph.

Lewis, Peter. 1978. *The Fifties*. Heineman, London.

Nathan, David. 1971. *The Laughtermakers, the quest for comedy*. Peter Owen, London.

Report of the Broadcasting Committee, 1949 (Beveridge Committee) HMSO Cmnd. 8116, 1951.

Report of the Broadcasting Committee, 1960 (Pilkington Committee) HMSO Cmnd. 1753, 1962.

Report of the Committee on the Future of Broadcasting (Annan Committee) HMNS Cmnd. 6753, 1977.

Report on Broadcasting in Everyday Life, Hilda Jennings and Winifred Gill on behalf of the BBC, 1939.

Ross, Duncan. Spring 1950. *The documentary in television. BBC Q.* **5**.

Scannell, G. P. 1979. *The realities of television, 1946–1955, Media, Culture and Society* **1** (1).

Tuchman, Gaye. ed. 1978. *Images of Women in the Mass Media*. Oxford University Press, Oxford.

Vaughan, Dai. 1978. *Television Documentary Usage*, BFI Television Monograph.

Wilson, Elizabeth. 1977. *Women and the Welfare State*. Tavistock, London.

Women's Studies Int. Quart., 1980, Vol. 3, pp. 29–39
Pergamon Press Ltd.   Printed in Great Britain

THE 'LIBERATED WOMAN' IN TELEVISION DRAMA

Helen Baehr

School of Communication, Polytechnic of Central London, 18–22 Riding House Street,
London, W1, U.K.

(*Accepted September* 1979)

Synopsis—The mass media set an agenda for public opinion. They select themes, items and points of view which tend to reinforce patriarchal culture. In this paper I look at the way the mass media, in particular a serious television drama series *Play for Today*, constructed and placed a stereotype of 'the liberated woman' on the media agenda. For a majority of the audience the two plays discussed represented a major source of information about ideas and issues central to the feminist movement. Feminism here, however, is co-opted by the medium and re-constructed into a stereotype of the liberated woman which is emptied of progressive meaning.*

'We can only understand culture if we understand the real social process on which it depends—I mean the process of incorporation. This dominant and effective culture is constantly active and adjusting and so we have to recognize that alternative opinions and attitudes and sense of the world can be accomodated and tolerated within this culture' (Williams, 1977).

The mass media have established a decisive and fundamental leadership in the production and transmission of patriarchal culture in contemporary society. They are more and more responsible for the construction and consumption of social knowledge and 'represent a key repository of available meanings which people draw on in their continuing attempts to make sense of their situation and find ways of acting within and against it' (Murdock, 1974). And yet culture is not a static system—it is a process, as Raymond Williams suggests, which is constantly changing to accommodate emergent alternative and oppositional meanings, values and practices. In this paper I want to try to examine the role the mass media, in particular 'serious' television drama, have played in accomodating and delegitimizing feminism and feminist issues through their construction of a stereotype of 'the liberated woman'.

THE POWER OF THE MASS MEDIA

Early researchers into the mass media spent a great number of years refuting their own hypothesis that the media have a direct behavioural effect on the audience (Lazarsfeld *et al.*, 1944). Research undertaken in America in the 1950s found instead that the power of the media was located within existing structures of social relationships (Lazarsfeld and Katz, 1955). 'Personal influence' and social variables such as age, social class, education—gender was not usually considered—were recognized as important intervening mechanisms operating between the mass communication message and the audience.

Through its empirical methodology, media sociology tended to define 'effect' narrowly in behaviourist terms highlighting the audience's apparent resistance to individual messages.

---

* My thanks to Karyn Kay and Gillian Dyer for their help.

This no-effects model has since come under severe criticism (Gitlin, 1978). That we cannot trace very precise causal connections between messages and effects should not dissolve the complex question of the power of the media. They occupy a central position in culture in two important ways. Firstly, contact with the various media provides the majority of the population with their dominant leisure activity[1] and secondly, the media constitute a main source of information about, and explanation of, social and political processes.[2] Structured closely to other powerful institutions, they help establish an order of priorities about a society's problems and objectives.

The media select items for attention and provide rankings of what is and is not important—in other words they 'set an agenda' for public opinion (McCombs and Shaw, 1972). The way the media choose themes, structure the dialogue and control the debate—a process which involves crucial omissions—is a major aspect of their influence. Many topics are excluded from the media news agenda: shopping, housework, having a baby (unless it is Princess Anne). News about women traditionally concentrates on aspects of their appearance, sexuality and domestic relations. Feminist research into the mass media has shown that women tend to be shown as submissive, passive and are portrayed largely in terms of their sexuality or domesticity while men tend to be shown as dominant, active and authoritative (Tuchman *et al.*, 1978; Janus, 1977; King and Stott, 1977; Sharpe, 1976; Busby, 1975). Males greatly outnumber females in prime-time television and in TV soap operas males are more likely to discuss professional matters while women discuss romantic relationships, health and domestic matters (Katzman, 1972). In TV advertisements women clean, launder and cook while men give the orders and advice and eat the meals (Cantor, 1974). Women are subject to 'symbolic annihilation' through their condemnation, trivialisation and absence in the mass media (Tuchman *et al.*, 1978).

Much of this research puts forward a reflection model of the media—that is, the media simply reflect the values of a society and the position of women in that society. Some work has turned the model on its head to suggest that media images themselves determine what women are: 'We think we should look more closely at how our attitudes are conditioned, and even manipulated by the media' (King and Stott, 1977). The media, however, do not simply reflect representations of women. They are one site of the construction of women's marginality in culture and are themselves a point of production of definitions (Cowie, 1978). The question of representation is a major problem here particularly as it relates to the issue of realism. In a useful survey of recent developments in feminist criticism, Christine Gledhill discusses the different theoretical approaches to the hybrid phenomenon of realism, aesthetic practices and female stereotypes (Gledhill, 1978).

ON THE MEDIA AGENDA

Earlier treatment by the media in the late sixties and early seventies discredited 'women's libbers' as being hostile, aggressive man-haters who lacked a sense of humour (Barr, 1977). Women's libbers appeared as a minority of women who stood apart, deviated, from the

---

[1] In Britain a government survey showed that watching TV was by far the most popular pastime. *Planning for Leisure*, 1969. HM Stationery Office London.
[2] In a recent survey 90 per cent of people asked about where they got information about what is going on in this country and in the world named TV, the newspapers and radio. Golding, P. 1974. *The Mass Media*. Longman, London.

majority of non-aggressive 'normal' women. They acquired a set of 'secondary status' attributes in press reports—they were described as lesbians, frigid and too ugly to get a man. More recently the Women's Liberation Movement has been co-opted onto the media agenda resulting in less hysterical coverage and according a degree of legitimate status to women's demands for 'equal rights'.

But the liberated woman constructed by the mass media is the woman who wants to get on in a man's world. Press reports of the first woman bullfighter, jet pilot, prime minister etc., describe women who have secured jobs that were formerly totally male preserves. 'Women's firsts' represent the success stories of equal opportunity defined by the law as the right of every woman. The new, independent, modern woman is portrayed as a woman who wants, and occasionally achieves, equal status with men. The mass media have helped set up a new majority/minority paradigm. Minority status has shifted away from independent, ambitious women to feminists who continue to question the very notion of equality within existing structures and who continue to be omitted and discredited in the media. Ironically when 'first women' are asked the inevitable question about their views on 'women's lib', they usually oblige by dissociating themselves from the Women's Movement: 'I am not terrifically Women's Lib; I simply ignore all these anti-attitudes. I am a conductor and just get on with it' (*Sunday Times* interview with orchestral conductor Jane Glover) (Barr, 1977).

George Gerbner observes the introduction onto American television of independent, powerful women who are portrayed as *enforcing* rather than challenging the laws that oppress them. They play policewomen, detectives or soldiers e.g. *Policewoman, Charlie's Angels* (Gerbner, 1978). These characters bear little resemblance to feminist aspirations— they usually end up needing to be rescued by their male partners. But the fact that heroic women have supplemented heroic men on the screen, points to the way in which the media have taken note of, and re-constructed, feminist issues. Here we see strong women re-constructed into redeemers of the patriarchy.

Over the last year, a British newspaper, *The Guardian*, has introduced a 'fortnightly column of feminist news and opinions' onto the woman's page. This ghettoisation places women's issues and feminism in a marginally depoliticized relation to the rest of the news. Another national newspaper marked 1978 as 'The Year of the Feminist' and went on to confuse films about women (directed by men) with 'films on feminist themes' (*The Observer*, December 31. 1978). Films like *The Turning Point, An Unmarried Woman* and *Julia* have packaged images of the new, independent, liberated woman for mass consumption. The 'new woman' is a new media cliché—the New Hollywood brand of feminism. In *An Unmarried Woman* independence stands for not capitulating too easily when Mr Right makes his inevitable appearance: 'It's the film's intention to put things "in fashion". So it's not really a question of feminism so much as it is seeing how its issues can be rephrased in the proper style' (Ehrenstein, 1978).

So particular images of feminism have already been 'sold' to the commercial culture— 'the assertive, ambitious woman is no longer an oddity but has become a new cultural type' (Cagan, 1978). The 'new woman' has just as much potential for being a profitable consumer as the 1950s 'traditional homemaker' described by Betty Friedan (Friedan, 1963). Female sexuality, often confused with female liberation, has become big business. There has been a multiplication of areas of the body accessible to marketability: 'What is happening is that a new definition of women's sexuality is being produced. It is a definition which produces new areas as sensual and equates that sensuality with work' (Coward, 1978). The work referred to involves the purchase of appliances, accessories and cosmetics and

Elizabeth Cagan argues that the new cultural type of the liberated woman has been manufactured to serve the commodity market of a capitalist economy:

'Thus, we begin to observe an increase in ads which feature female models and address themselves to the aspirations of women for the "good life" but which in actuality might just have easily been written for the male market.' (Cagan, 1978).

Cagan stresses the need for the Women's Movement to 'divorce itself from this image and distinguish its own approaches to liberation.' However, within a media structure heavily influenced and determined by market forces, the means of producing and disseminating alternative media artefacts and progressive images of women remain severely limited. The producers of a television series planned to show the wife of one leading character as 'a middle-aged housewife worried by her three children.' But she never appeared on the screen. Instead they decided to play safe and the wife appeared as a slim, sexy blonde: 'Realism had taken another knock. It all helped the ratings though' (Elliott, 1973).

THE 'LIBERATED WOMAN' IN TELEVISION DRAMA

Even British broadcasting has responded to women as the 'new growth industry'. There has been a significant increase in the past few years in the number of television programmes focusing on women and women's issues. Programmes have included a series about 'exceptional women', women at war, documentaries and dramas on the menopause, pre-menstrual tension, rape, working mothers and abortion. Scheduling has often conferred minority status to these programmes by allocating them to off-peak, late-night viewing. A drama/documentary series *A Woman's Place* was reshown on BBC 1 at 11.55 pm on a Sunday evening.

One early introduction of 'the liberated woman' to the British television audience came in the BBC's serious drama slot *Play for Today*. Within the short space of four months in 1976/1977 three new plays, all of which centred around characters and themes related to women's liberation, were broadcast. 'A sight of the times' wrote one television critic (Alan Coren in *The Times*, January 26, 1977). The three plays—*Housewives' Choice*, *Do as I Say* and *Mother Song*—were written, produced and directed by men.[3]

Play for Today has, since its inception in the 1960s, exerted considerable influence in constituting the 'serious issues of the day.' It represents the 'quality' television play with a social conscience—'*Play for Today* has re-established the single play as the contemporary voice of Britain' (*Daily Mail*, February 4, 1978). One of the few women producers involved in the series describes their intention to present plays 'with a message, full of gutsy contemporaneity' (Shubick, 1975). A recent play in the series provided an account of wife-battering which effectively put the issue on the media agenda and provoked a wide response from television reviewers (*Don't be Silly* by Rachel Billington, broadcast on July 24, 1979). An outstanding play produced in the 1960s was a moving account of homelessness and is publicly acknowledged as having been instrumental in setting up 'Shelter' an organization for the homeless (*Cathy Come Home*, 1966).

---

[3] *Housewives' Choice* by Roy Kendall, producer Ken Trodd, broadcast October 18, 1976. *Do as I Say* by Charles Wood, producer Graeme McDonald, broadcast January 25, 1977. *Mother Song* by John Hopkins, producer Mark Shivas, broadcast February 8, 1977. In this paper I shall refer to the first two plays. *Mother Song* was a play about a single mother and although it touched on themes drawn from the women's movement, it did not include a portrayal of 'the liberated woman.'

The fact that television drama is judged to perform an important social and aesthetic function in the eyes of media practioners and critics is confirmed by the fact that the entire 1977 Edinburgh International Television Festival was devoted to a discussion of the effectiveness and 'truthfulness' of realist and naturalist modes of presentation. Several *Plays for Today* are regarded as television 'classics' and a retrospective of selected plays is scheduled for screening at the London National Film Theatre later this year. In a further attempt to save the plays for posterity the publishers Eyre Methuen have decided to publish the texts of nine of the plays produced in 1979.

Play for Today encourages writers, producers, directors and actors to explore new topics and new forms of expression. Tony Garnett, a producer in the series, explained how in the 1960s he and his colleagues explicitly set out to find material that broke with the conventions of 'middle-brow' theatre:

> 'We wanted to find a new kind of writer . . . people who'd never written anything before but who seemed to have something to say . . . some of them wrote things which meant we had to make them on location, in real places' (Hudson, 1972).

Although the series defines itself as presenting innovatory plays its writers are drawn from established theatre writers or from a relatively small pool of experienced television writers. This, added to the 'old-tie network' that exists amongst television practitioners, works to exclude many women writers who have not had the same opportunities to establish themselves. On the rare occasions when a feminist writer has gained access there remains the problem of handing over production decisions to the 'professionals' who, at senior executive level in television, are invariably men. One play about lesbianism which was written by a woman—*The Other Woman* by Watson Gould broadcast in January 1976— caused a woman artist who had contributed to the production, to write a public apology 'to all lesbians, women artists and members of the Women's Movement for having painted the pictures for the BBC *Play for Today*. It is very obvious that the play was manipulated by people, who, whether they realize it or not, are totally insensitive and ignorant about and feel very threatened by lesbianism.' (Letter from Catherine Nicholson to the *Evening Standard*, January 12, 1976). More work needs to be done in this area but it appears to be a common feature for women working in television to experience particular difficulties in dealing with male colleagues, male senior executives, male crews and time slot allocations when engaged in making their own programmes.[4]

Play for Today has a long tradition of showing plays 'with a message' and the inclusion of women's liberation on its agenda marked a rare opportunity to accord media legitimacy to feminist issues. This chance was, however, lost. Instead we saw two plays—*Housewives' Choice* and *Do as I Say*—which constructed the liberated woman in a way which effectively worked to delegitimize feminist issues and the feminist movement.

---

[4] Television companies have 'window-dressed' their sets by employing women newsreaders, presenters etc., giving the impression that one woman completes equality of opportunity for all women. Although women have become more visible on camera, they are still a marked absence in the real decision-making, producer and executive level jobs. See *Patterns of Discrimination*, 1975 a report compiled by the Association of Cinematograph and Television Technicians and *Women in broadcasting: de jure, de facto* in this issue.

The experience of women employed in television was the subject of a conference on *Women's Issues and TV* held in May 1979 at the Polytechnic of Central London and it is from my observations there that I note the particular difficulties faced by women in the industry.

HOUSEWIVES' CHOICE

In this *Play for Today* the liberated woman is portrayed by Marcia who is middle-class and 'lives in a very respectable neighbourhood' (descriptions and dialogue taken from original script).

Marcia is surrounded by homely comforts and domestic appliances and 'has just had the offer of something really rather nice. In books'. The opening shot of her shows her dressed in a jump suit and playing the cello. She has a short 'boyish' haircut and a deep voice. Her physical appearance, combined with the legs astride position, immediately brings into question her 'femininity'. Marcia, once married to an American businessman, now divorced, has an 11-month-old daughter, androgenously called 'Sam'.

Marcia, to her disadvantage, is juxtaposed with the other central character, Joyce. Joyce is everything Marcia is not. She is married, childless (longing to have a baby) and homeless. She and her unemployed husband (Eric) are living in their car. To get a child-minding job looking after Sam, Joyce lies to Marcia pretending to have a home and children of her own. Marcia sets out to raise Joyce's feminist consciousness. She does this by using jargon and appearing ridiculous:

'One day we shall create our own Garden of Eden with no more drudgery and no more falls. We everywhere: one universal consciousness'.

One television critic wrote: 'Frances de la Tour, who plays Marcia, was selflessly good as the hard, incessantly opinionated divorcee *preaching* women's rights to helpless, homeless home help Joyce.' (*Sunday Telegraph* October 24, 1976). The same reviewer refers to Marcia's 'comfy middle-class attitudinizing'. Joyce does indeed appear to be helpless—but her problems, as constructed within the play, stem from her lack of all that Marcia attacks.

The introduction to the play states that: 'Joyce seems to be the average housewife and her problems are not the ones Marcia is determined to solve' (*Radio Times*, October 18, 1976). Joyce wants desperately to become 'an average housewife' with a husband who has a job, a house of her own and a family. Contrasted to Joyce's needs, Marcia's feminist ideas are *not* those facing the average housewife. Unaware of Joyce's true predicament, Marcia's feminism comes across as an abstraction, bourgeois, unrelated to 'real' problems or the real world:

'The point is Joyce, we've got to break out of our stereotypes . . . the set two-dimensional roles—housewife, mother, whore, you know . . . that the male supremacy things makes us play. Would you like some more coffee?'

It seems all very well for Marcia to 'preach' women's rights surrounded as she is by all material comforts and a husband who pays: 'Don't worry' she tells Joyce, 'my husband is paying the bills.' Marcia's feminism is placed on the level of a middle-class privilege and pure self-indulgence. The audience's sympathy is drawn towards 'helpless' Joyce who wants nothing more than the chance to have her own family and home. Marcia's concept of the Garden of Eden will not solve that problem. Joyce needs to *become* the average housewife to solve her problems. The average housewife apparently has no problems! In the play feminist concerns remain too theoretical and 'middle-class' to have any application to the real problems and situation facing women's everyday lives.

Marcia to Eric:

'One day . . . one day we actually *will* be liberated. One day there will be no division of labour, no job discrimination—one day childbirth will not be painful. One day, when your anatomy is no longer your destiny, art and technology will merge and create an androgynous culture, a new reality.'

Coming from the character of Marcia, these words and ideals—taken by the male playwright directly from the Women's Movement—are emptied of any significant meaning. Feminism is reduced to Marcia's armchair dogmatism. She spouts feminist theory—but her life-style denies its practice:

Eric: 'Your push button world's all very well but you don't have to work in the factories that make the buttons!'
Marcia: 'Look, mate when the revolution comes everyone will have to make the washing machines and the TV's.'
Eric: 'Except for the clever people like you, who're all for it in theory but'll find a way of getting out of it in practice.'

Marcia's indictment of men and marriage stands in contradiction to the example of Eric's relationship with Joyce. Joyce and Eric are happy together despite their 'real' problems. Their marriage survives—even flourishes under—unemployment, childlessness and home-lessness. Marriage and the family are the only true values.

Joyce to Eric:

'Oh, love, don't worry. It's going to be alright. We'll have our own place and kids too, with any luck, and you'll have a decent job. It'll be alright. It'll be lovely.'

Their happy marriage stands as an affirmation of the family that Marcia condemns. Marcia's feminism, here confined to 'women's rights', operates at the level of metaphysics.

Eric to Marcia:

'If you weren't so busy with women's rights, you'd see there's a lot more wrong with the world.'

DO AS I SAY

In January 1977 the BBC held a 'rape week' (my term). It included a *Play for Today* about a rape—*Do as I Say*—and a studio discussion 'between people familiar with the problems involved' (*Radio Times*, January 22–28, 1977). Pressure from the Women's Movement for rape to be treated as a serious subject and the passing of the Sexual Offences (Amendment) Act[5] must have played a significant part in putting rape onto the television agenda at that time.

The studio discussion—*Act of Rape*—presents an interesting example of the ways in which the media structure the dialogue and control the debate of the issues they select to cover. The people 'familiar' with rape who were invited to speak on the panel included two male Members of Parliament, a male judge, a male police surgeon, a woman police officer, a male psychiatrist, a woman author of a book on rape—'professionals in the field'—and two rape victims. The programme was billed as 'exploring the attitudes we (sic) have made many victims suffer unnecessarily before the courts' (*Radio Times*).

---

[5] The Sexual Offences (Amendment) Act passed in 1976 changed the law on rape in an attempt to end the practice at rape trials of submitting the victim to a gruelling and well-publicized examination of her personal life.

At one point one of the rape victims was asked to describe her experience of reporting to the police after she had been raped:

'I had to wait four hours before the police doctor could come. There are some women watching this programme now who are going to be raped; that is a very high statistical probability. And if anyone is raped, don't go to the police.'

The rape victim is cut short by the chairperson: 'Please let the police have some right of reply.' This makes her statement appear as an aggressive, unreasonable intervention. The policewoman is conferred her right to present the point of view of authority. It is difficult to imagine the same right of reply being granted to the rape victims. The discussion takes place within the terms of reference of the 'experts' who concentrate on changing the laws and 'attitudes' ignoring the causes, long-term effects and violent nature of rape. The rape victims (the non-experts) are there to provide their individual, personal accounts but it is the decision-makers in society that represent the 'impartial' and 'objective' analysis of the issues.

The medical examination undergone after a rape is described by the medical expert on the panel and not by the women who have had direct experience of it. This is what Becker has called the 'hierarchy of credibility' whereby those in positions of power are asked for their opinions about controverisal topics and are likely to have their definitions accepted— because of their authoritative position and often because their definitions are the *only* ones made available (Becker, 1972). It is these people—politicians, trade union leaders, doctors, the police, employers—who become the 'primary definers' of topics and events (Hall, 1978). There is a structured 'over-accessing' to the media of those in powerful positions so that it is the politicians, the lawyers and the police who control the debate on rape in this programme. In the same way the abortion issue has until now been publicly structured by the Church and the medical profession around the issues of the moral and health implications of abortion and not around a woman's right to choose.

The play *Do as I Say* was broadcast with the warning that: 'Because of the subject some of the scenes will be necessarily explicit' (*Radio Times*, January 25, 1977). The rape scene was in fact explicitly civilized. Daphne is raped in her own home, by a man who offers his name, invites his victim to choose a comfortable spot, offers her a cushion and gives her time to go to the bathroom to insert her diaphragm! All through the rape there are cuts to Daphne's television set which is showing a cricket match and a running commentary filled with sexual innuendo 'five slips and a gulley.' The warning indicates the media's definition of rape as a sexually explicit act—not a crime of violence often combined with robbery, weapons and other sexual acts besides that of vaginal penetration (Brownmiller, 1975). This play, though responding to pressure from feminists to get rape discussed seriously, has co-opted the subject and completely undermined its serious and violent nature: 'Outrage of rape has lighter moments.' wrote one TV critic (*Daily Telegraph*, January 26, 1977).

The theme of the liberated woman is taken up again. Hilary is Daphne's American neighbour who comes over to see her after the rape. Hilary appears dressed in jeans, hair in ringlets and legs astride in Daphne's doorway—'Oh, wow! You lucked out, eh?' She tells Daphne her legal rights under the circumstances and refers to Daphne's 'truly horrendous situation—this morbid trip'. She expounds to an incredulous Daphne much as Marcia 'preached' to Joyce, that 'you can rape a body but you can't rape a pysche' and that she 'must get it together' and 'erase the bad news, be here now'. Her offers of help are emptied of meaning by her unwelcomed (untimely) sexual advance to Daphne.

Hilary, like Marcia, uses jargon—'Hilary talked a prose style strongly reminiscent, in its rhetorical viscosity, of the dedicatory passage to *The Female Eunuch*' (Clive James in *The Observer*, January 30, 1977). Another reviewer described Hilary as 'a with-it American who could, and did, take 78 words to say 'Yes'' (Richard Last in *The Daily Telegraph*, January 26, 1977).

SO WHAT'S NEW?

Television's agenda-setting function confers on it the power to provide a repository of available meanings which people can draw on to make sense of events and issues which are often removed from their direct experience. It is unlikely (and a sad reflection) that the majority of the television audience will have direct experience of the Women's Movement or feminism which places these plays in a strong position as a major—with the paucity of air time given over to the subject possibly the *only*—source of information about feminist issues. In a study of the media's news presentations of race, white respondents living in areas of high and low immigration differed in their descriptions of the racial situation in Britain during the period from 1963 to 1970 (Hartmann and Husband, 1974). But, at the same time, and this is the crucial point, the authors argue that their evidence tends to indicate that *all* respondents shared a common overall definition derived from media news coverage, of coloured immigrants constituting a 'problem'. This finding points to the centrality of 'media-relayed' meanings in providing pervasive and authoritative definitions of social situations and issues.

Drama provides one of the largest and most popular categories of television output and in the case of British commercial television, drama programmes dominate both the schedules and the ratings.[6] The single play, of which *Play for Today* is the most prestigious, is regarded by both the BBC and the Independent Broadcasting Authority as essential to support the kind of original writing 'which will do more than simply entertain and may work at a number of levels and enlarge the awareness and sympathies of its audiences' (IBA, 1977/1978). There is some evidence to suggest that play audiences do gain from the experience of viewing particular plays and can often be moved and disturbed (McQuail, 1970).

Although television drama covers a wide spectrum of topics in contemporary society,[7] by no means all social life is there. There are important questions that still need to be asked about the institutional and professional practices within which drama selects and excludes both topics and modes of representation. There is also the difficult question that Gledhill raises about the various ways people may 'read' the mass media and how far such readings are made through identifications and recognitions. This problem is highlighted in her discussion of what constitutes a feminist reading and the possibility of replacing traditional female stereotypes:

'Stereotypes do not vanish on the production of an image of real women, or of Feminist aspiration. They are materialized in the way society is structured and the way we live our lives: they are part of our reality' (Gledhill, 1978).

Housewives' Choice and *Do as I Say* are examples of some of the first presentations of the liberated woman stereotype on British television. Since then we have seen the film industry's

---

[6] Drama and drama series form the largest part of commercial television's output. The range of drama s very wide and includes single plays, anthologies, adaptations and serials. For precise figures see the *Independent Broadcasting Authority's Annual Report and Accounts*.

[7] Topics covered by *Play for Today* over the last couple of years include nuclear energy, alcoholism, Fascism, political dissidents, mastectomy and wife-battering.

attempt to exploit the independent woman theme and a small, but increasing, number of television drama/documentaries on women and women's issues. Marcia and Hilary illustrate one important way in which the challenges of feminism have been ideologically accomodated by the mass media through a patriarchal production of 'the liberated woman.'

Both women are portrayed as pretentious, overly intense propagandists, pre-occupied with 'women's rights' to the exclusion of the 'real' problems of the world. They are 'with-it' implying that their feminist concerns are a fad—a phase they will grow out of. Being a feminist is 'in' but feminists cannot be taken too seriously because they will soon be 'out'. Marcia and Hilary swear, stride across the set and are angry i.e. 'unfeminine'. Hilary is a caricature of an American Consciousness III hippy. Marcia describes life in the United States:

> 'You must understand the whole culture was designed to keep women in the home. God, the TV commercials! Happy cornflake families with a feminine mum and a masculine car. Buy, buy, buy! And stay at home so that you'll know what to go on buying in order to go on being happy!'

A study of the press coverage of the Vietnam demonstrations that took place in London in October 1968 adds a dimension to this use of the American reference. The British press at the time made a great deal of the fact that the leading organizers of the march were not English (Murdock, 1973). By using the focus of 'foreign agitators'—e.g. Tariq Ali and Abhimanya Manchanda—the conflict appeared to come from outside the consensus. In much the same way, Marcia and Hilary's 'obsession' with women's rights appears to bear little or no relevance to Joyce and Daphne. In both cases British society remains apparently free from any permanently structured conflict of interests from within. Feminism here is imported from America and marked out as 'foreign' so distancing the audience from its issues. It is discredited in British eyes which still look to America as a major exporter of all the worst aspects of materialism, excess and inferior culture.

Both television critics and audiences look to *Play for Today* to present plays 'with a message'. *Housewives' Choice* and *Do as I Say* illustrate the way feminist issues and women's 'liberation' are co-opted onto the media agenda where they are accomodated within a patriarchal discourse which empties them of progressive meaning. The themes and issues of feminism are drawn on and presented in a way that leads to the ultimate re-affirmation of the patriarchal family—a critique of which lies at the core of feminist ideology. Marcia and Hilary are rendered unnatural, ridiculous and wrong.

REFERENCES

ACTT, 1975. *Patterns of Discrimination*. London.
Barr, Pat. 1977. Newspapers. In: Stott, M. and King, J. eds. *Is this your Life?* Virago, London.
Becker, H. 1972. Whose side are we on? In: Douglas, J. D. ed. *The Relevance of Sociology*. Appleton-Century-Crofts, New York.
Brownmiller, Susan, 1975. *Against Our Will*. Martin Secker & Warburg, London.
Busby, Linda. Autumn 1975. Sex-role research on the mass media. *J. Communication*.
Cagan, Elizabeth. 1978. The selling of the women's movement. *Social Policy* 8, 4–12.
Cantor, Muriel, 1974. Comparison of tasks and roles of males and females in commercials aired by WRC-TV during composite week. In: *Women in the Wasteland Fight Back: A Report on the Image of Women Portrayed in TV Programming*. NOW, National Capitol Area Chapter.
Coward, Ros. 1978. Sexual liberation and the family. *M/F* 1, 7–23.
Cowie, Liz. 1978. Woman as sign. *M/F* 1, 49–63.
Eddings, Barbara. 1980. Women in broadcasting: *de jure, de facto. Women's Studies Int. Quart.* 3 (1), 1–13.

Ehrenstein, D. 1978. Melodrama and the New Woman. *Film Comment* **14**, (5), 59–62.

Elliott, J. 1973. *Mogul: the making of a myth*. Longman, London.

Friedan, Betty. 1963. *The Feminine Mystique*. Victor Gollancz, London.

Gerbner, George. 1978. The dynamics of cultural resistance. In: Tuchman, G. Daniels, A. and Benet, D. eds. *Hearth and Home*. Oxford University Press, Oxford.

Gitlin, Todd. 1978. Media sociology: The dominant paradigm. *Theory and Society* **6** (2), 205–253.

Gledhill, Christine. 1978. Recent developments in feminist criticism. *Q. Rev. Film Studies* **3** (4), 457–493.

Golding, Peter. 1974. *The Mass Media*, Longman, London.

HM Stationery Office London, 1969. *Planning for Leisure*.

Hall, S. 1978. *Policing the Crisis*. Macmillan, London.

Hartmann, P. and Husband, C. 1974. *Racism and the Mass Media*. Davis-Poynter, London.

Hudson, R. 1972. Television in Britain: description and dissent. *Theatre Q.* **11**, 19.

Independent Broadcasting Authority Annual Report and Accounts, 1977–78.

Janus, Noreen. 1977. Research on sex-roles in the mass media: toward a critical approach. *Insurgent Sociologist* **VII** (3), 19–32.

Katzman, N. 1972. TV soap operas: what's been going on anyway? *Public Opinion Q.* **36** (2).

King, J. and Stott, M. 1977. *Is this Your Life? Images of Women in the Media*. Virago, London.

Lazarsfeld, P. and Katz, E. 1955. *Personal Influence: the Part Played by People in the flow of Mass Communication*. Glencoe Free Press.

Lazarsfeld, P., Berelson, B. and Gaudet, H. 1944. *The People's Choice: How the Voter Makes up his Mind in a Presidential Campaign*, Duell, Sloan and Pearce, New York.

McCombs, M. and Shaw, D. 1972. The agenda-setting function of the mass media. *Public Opinion Q.* **36** (2), 176–187.

McQuail, D. 1970. The audience for Television plays. In: Tunstall, J. ed. *Media Sociology*. Constable, London.

Murdock, G. 1973. Political deviance: the press presentation of a militant mass demonstration. In: Cohen, S. and Young, J. eds. *The Manufacture of News. Deviance, Social Problems and the Mass Media*. Constable, London.

Murdock, G. 1974. Mass communication and the construction of meaning. In: Armistead, N. ed. *Reconstructing Social Psychology*. Penguin, Harmondsworth.

Sharpe, Sue. 1976. *'Just Like a Girl' How Girls learn to be Women*. Virago, London.

Shubick, Irene, 1975. *Play for Today: The Evolution of Television Drama*. Davis-Poynter, London.

Tuchman, Gaye, Daniels, A. and Benet, D. 1978. *Hearth and Home. Images of Women in the Mass Media*. Oxford University Press, Oxford.

Williams, Raymond. 1977. *Marxism and Literature*. Oxford University Press, Oxford.

Women's Studies Int. Quart., 1980, Vol. 3, pp. 41–54
Pergamon Press Ltd.   Printed in Great Britain

WOMEN AND RADIO

ANNE KARPF

33 King Henry's Road, London N.W.3, U.K.

(*Accepted October* 1979)

Synopsis—The relationship between women and radio has been greatly neglected by the women's movement. This is unfortunate because radio is bound up with women's lives more than most other media. Women are under-represented as contributors in most areas of radio.* Afternoon radio plays, phone-in and medical programmes, and magazine programmes—all tend to present images of nuclear families with fulfilled women at their centre. In the past few years, some alternatives have been initiated, from Rome's feminist Radio Donna, to America's WOMN–1220, a commercial women's radio station. In Britain, there has been a successful local radio series raising issues important to housebound women with children. And the Women's Radio Workshop has just started making feminist radio programmes which it hopes will be broadcast on local radio.

While virtually all of the mass-media have come under feminist scrutiny in the past few years, radio has got off scot-free. Academics and women's groups have been diligently monitoring television, cinema, and the press: decoding signs of sexism, uncovering masculinist ideology, and promoting feminist alternatives. Yet radio, the medium which permeates women's lives more than any other, has been largely ignored.

Indeed, apart from one chapter in a book on images of women in the media (Ross, 1977), there appears to be no critique of British radio from a feminist perspective in print. This is a grave omission: it means that radio has been exempted from the kind of pressure and lobbying which often result from exposure of bias and distortion. Indeed, the very absence of vocal criticism implies that all's well with the medium, and encourages a complacent attitude to the status quo.

It is interesting that the BBC, always very industrious in its research, has done none whatsoever on women listeners (aside from the normal breakdown of listening figures as part of Audience Research), nor has it carried out more than minimal research on its employment of women. The Independent Broadcasting Authority (IBA), the body which regulates the independent local radio stations (ILR) has been hardly more interested. They have done little research apart from some limited surveying of listeners' attitudes to women presenters (IBA, 1977), and some more extensive current research (not yet published).

One can interpret this in two ways. It is not fanciful to suggest that the lack of interest on the part of official bodies is reinforced by the apparent indifference of the women's movement. This indifference stems, in turn, from the neglect of radio as a medium in British society. The BBC, for example, broadcast 980 plays on radio last year, each of which could probably fill a West End theatre for a year, yet between them they gleaned no more than a

---

* This is especially true of women broadcasting in daytime networked programmes which are designed to maintain the illusion of housewifely contentment which a woman presenter might rupture.

handful of newspaper reviews. And though 500 of them were new, original radio plays, there is no chair or lectureship of radio drama in the country.[1]

So it is scarcely surprising that if the medium in general is thus ignored, its special relationship with women should be even less examined. The unfortunate result is that radio continues to seem to the general public—to a greater degree than television, I would suggest—to be a medium that can be taken neat: as a source of education, information, and entertainment, rather than as a creator of a distinct ideology and a perpetrator of powerful images of women.

The British Broadcasting Corporation (BBC) operates four national networks (originally, there were three, designed to appeal to three different social classes).

Radio 1, which has the largest audience, was started in 1967 as the BBC's answer to the illegal pirate radio pop stations. It is almost entirely pop music, most of it mainstream chart-toppers, and its audience is typically under 30.

Radio 2 is MOR (middle-of-the-road), mainly popular older style light music, with an audience aged 30–49.

Radio 3 is mainly classical music during the day, drama and talks in the evening, with the smallest audience of all, typically middle-aged.

Radio 4 is the news, current affairs, and speech network and broadcasts most of the BBC's drama (Singer 1979).

The BBC also operates 20 local radio stations (started in 1967, and with a few new ones now being set up), as well as Scottish, Welsh, and Northern Ireland regional services. The Independent Broadcasting Authority oversees 19 commercially-financed local radio stations, known as ILR (Independent Local Radio), started in 1973, with 9 new ones in the process of being set up and a further 15 stations announced.

Radio is a particularly important medium for women to analyse because it is one which is especially shaped to attract them. Although housebound women watch television during the day, this is only during the afternoon, as there is as yet only very limited morning television in Britain, and evening programming is directed at a mixed audience. Radio, however, begins when the houseworking day starts, and can accompany every stage of the day until the television goes on in the evening. So for some women, all their listening takes place when they are alone: the radio is their only companion. This gives radio a power which virtually no other medium has, and also an intimacy.

Certainly, radio has an innate intimacy: individuals often possess their own set, while a television is more likely to be a shared 'family' one. And a 'tranny' is portable, so it can follow its owner into a variety of rooms and occupations. which adds to its personal quality. This is reflected in the timbres and tones which emanate from radio: disc jockeys and presenters often adopt a more intimate, familiar manner than they would in an equivalent TV programme.

It is a commonplace that people rarely listen to the radio without doing something else at the same time—domestic chores, for example. This is also true of much television watching. But radio is the only medium where this is built into its very ideology, and is a stated, acknowledged part of much of the programming, as we will see later on. Therefore radio occupies a very special relationship with women's lives, in that it is an explicit accompaniment to them—a commentary, or a counterpoint. This is sensitively conveyed by Micheline

---

[1] As cited by Ian Rodger in a letter to *New Society*, August 9, 1979.

Wandor in her short story *Radio Times* (Wandor, 1978), in which a single mother plays out her life with the radio constantly on, and the values coming from the set constantly rub up against her own experience of reality.

Perhaps the most persuasive reason that we must begin to take this medium seriously is that it is potentially the one most capable of being subverted towards feminist ends. It is not surprising that in past revolutions or coups, the radio station has been the first institution to be seized. Radio's combination of immediacy and simple technology, which permits effective broadcasting with only a low level of professional skill, renders it a medium especially amenable to non-professional access.

The British broadcasting system has a redoubtable history of resisting subversion. It is based on a duopoly, consisting of the BBC and the IBA. The BBC operates according to a Charter which details its objects and responsibilities. It is funded by the television licence fee, which also pays for its radio services (the radio licence was abolished in 1971) and which is fixed by Government. The IBA is regulated by an Act of Parliament and awards, renews, or denies franchises for ILR stations to private commercial companies (Lewis, 1978).

As becomes evident, Britain has been denied the pluralism in broadcasting which exists in countries like the United States, Canada, and Australia. In spite of demands by groups like ComCom, the Community Communications Group, for truly local, decentralized community radio (Community Communications Group, 1977), the situation remains that only those under the aegis of the BBC or IBA can run a radio station. ComCom wants to see a third force in British broadcasting: non-profit (unlike ILR), and truly local (unlike the BBC stations, whose policy and funds are centrally allocated). The Home Office is the government department which handles broadcasting (along with prisons) and any form of radio, whether air or cable, requires a licence from them, if it is not to contravene the Wireless Telegraphy Act, 1949. Hence, with the present situation, there could be no feminist radio station in Britain, unless initiated by the BBC or awarded a franchise by the IBA. The only alternative is piracy.

The pattern of women's employment in British radio is uneven, to say the least. They predominate in traditional female areas: 'caring' or domestic programmes, and the arts. They are a marked presence on Radio 4, the network which is heavily speech-oriented, with features, plays, and discussion programmes, and with a large middle-class and older audience. The Controller of the network is a woman, Monica Sims, and there are many women presenters and producers of Radio 4's documentary and magazine programmes—on education, the disabled, etc.—which emanate from CAMP, the Current Affairs and Magazine Programmes section. Women producers and presenters also run *Woman's Hour*, the afternoon magazine programme broadcast each weekday for 'women at home', Apart from its first few months in 1946, it has always been presented and produced by women.

But women are demonstrably absent from other BBC programme areas: they infrequently host phone-ins (except those, like *Tuesday Call*, run by the Woman's Hour Unit), but never quizzes or chat shows, or programmes where the chairperson marshalls conflicting opinions. They are newsreaders (after much management resistance), but rarely news commentators.

Drama is an area commonly supposed to attract women, yet out of 25 BBC drama producers based in London, only five are women, and only one (Liane Aukin) has children. Ms Aukin is very conscious of the fact that she is the only woman in the department having to juggle her public and private commitments.

'If I try to talk about it, it seems so personal, and as if I'm labelling women as "problems". If there were more women here, and women with children, we could get together and do something about it. And it would also encourage other women with children to work here' (personal interview).

According to the Annan Committee Report on the future of broadcasting, the most major review of British broadcasting since the 1962 Pilkington Report, 'only since 1973, when they carried out a study into the recruitment and advancement of women, have the BBC arranged for all vacancies to be open to both men and women. They told us that by 1974 there had been a small increase in the number of women occupying top jobs, and 40 per cent of those in training for further advancement at that time were women. Even so, only 12 per cent of the BBC's management and production staff were women' (Annan, 1977). Presumably, these figures refer to both TV and radio. The BBC has no creche.*

Women also occupy a tokenist position as guests and contributors on chat or discussion programmes, which are powerful methods by which the media help emphasize opinion-formers. Perhaps the best known of such programmes is Radio 4's *Any Questions*, a weekly panel of celebrities who give their opinion on political and social issues connected with the week's events in answers to questions from a live audience in a local hall. It regularly fields one woman with three men. Ex-Director General of the BBC, Charles Curran, argued on a phone-in that the ratio of one woman to four men 'represents the participation of women in public life' (Ross, 1977). As Ross comments, 'he was not concerned about reflecting the ratio of women in our society'.

On this subject there was also critical evidence submitted to the Annan Committee.

'Women in Media argued that although women were now appearing in more television and radio programmes, they rarely took the lead and were invariably confined to "women's interest" . . . Some of us felt that there is an in-built assumption that a man knows how to address an audience composed of men and women, but a woman does not. We also noticed that when there were discussions on radio or television there would be a token woman with three men, but that women would equal the number of men or even outnumber them, only when the topic dealt with women or children. No wonder women complain' (Annan, 1977).

Independent local radio, as befits a more recent phenomenon, has given greater opportunities to women. Capital Radio, one of the two London ILR stations, for example, is eager to list its 'on-air' women, who include Anna Raeburn, Jane Walmsley, Maggie Norden, and Gillian Reynolds—12 in all. Yet these are all contributors and it is the daily presenters who are the life-blood of a station and promote and maintain its identity—but of these, Capital has only one woman.

Moreover, the women it does employ all work in speech programmes (though Maggie Norden does use music in her teenage magazine programme *Hullabuloo*) and predominantly minority interest broadcasting. As Jane Walmsley said:

'We do tend to present the talks programmes—and we tend to be university graduates. The women here are sorry there aren't more women, but we feel it's difficult to make out

---

* When, elsewhere, a senior BBC broadcasting executive was asked why there were no women on his level in policy-making jobs, he replied: 'Of course we have women in senior management—we all have wives' (Ross, 1977).

a logical case—to point out areas which aren't covered, which would be if there were more women' (personal interview).

Radio, like any other male-dominated medium, has witnessed the familiar sight of professional women, having struggled into elevated positions, defending the existing structure with more conviction than a man. For example Mary Goldring, one of the few women news commentators, believes that:

'My particular brand of current affairs, which is economic and technical, is a most sexless profession: people don't mind if you're a man, woman, or a chimpanzee. It doesn't particularly matter that many women aren't doing it, because if there were, it wouldn't alter the way in which it is done—you're simply not dealing with material where it matters, you're dealing with something analytic' (personal interview).

She expresses a common notion (to some extent self-fulfilling: if she does it like men do, no one *will* be able to tell the difference) that there are various areas of life (especially the analytic—as opposed, it is implied, to the emotional) which have escaped masculinist ideology, that are somehow neutral. It is significant that this idea should find favour in the BBC, since it is closely related to that other preferred BBC idea, that of 'objectivity' in broadcasting—that there is a Truth that can be extracted from the morass of partiality by the acute pincers of the Corporation.

There are, however, producers who contest that view. Liane Aukin says:

'I think it matters a great deal that there are more women producers. Finally, if you are going to reflect all tastes and opinions of women as a group—though they often overlap with men's—women do need to be stronger represented when it comes to the editorial choice of material. Even if they're just a presence, it makes it harder to ignore them' (personal interview).

Such a view, of course, can be manipulated into a form of biological determinism. Even if it is suggested that it is women's common experience (cultural rather than biological) which gives them a particular perspective, it is a viewpoint which is frequently summoned to justify typecasting women in traditional women's areas.

In any case, there is a real danger in conducting the debate about women in radio on this level: the distribution of jobs to middle-class women should not be the issue—after jobs for the boys, jobs for the girls? Especially, as we have already seen, successful women (or those of any oppressed group) often deliberately disassociate themselves from their peer group.

What we should examine is the relationship between the employment of women in certain areas of broadcasting, and the images of women produced by those broadcasts. The best example is strip programming, the continuous mix of music and chat hosted by DJs which make up the morning schedules of BBC Radios 1 (pop music) and 2 (middle-of-the-road music) and the ILR schedules. Is there a connection between the type of product offered, and the fact that there is not more than a handful of female DJs of strip-shows in Britain? The causality is probably not that the DJs determine the product, but rather that the choice of product determines the DJs.

The BBC, which has not one single daily female DJ, offers a typically muddled defence. Doreen Davies, Executive Producer of Radio 1, says that they are rarely approached by women with appropriate experience (of discos, night-clubs, or journalism). But 'at the BBC there is no discrimination: it depends who is best for the job, it doesn't matter what sex or colour they are' (personal interview).

At the same time she says:

'the audience does tend to accept men more readily. There are more women and girl listeners than men, and you cannot deny that a young girl (sic) with a couple of small children at home will more easily relate to a man. It's like having a male friend in the house while the husband's away without the obvious repercussions'.

This sexual undertone is a pronounced aspect of all the strip-shows. David Hamilton, who presents a daily Radio 2 show, has said in an interview in the *Daily Mail* in 1973

'I try to talk to one person. I've got this picture of a young woman, a housewife, young or young at heart. She's probably on her own virtually all day. She's bored with the routine of housework and with her own company and for her I'm the slightly cheeky romantic visitor' (Ross, 1977).

This is the key to the sandwich of patter and music which fills daytime programmes: the risque innuendo fired by male DJs to a supposedly all-female public could not be replicated by a female DJ, even to a male audience, because it would denote a level of sexual aggression unacceptable in a woman. Radio critic Gillian Reynolds recognized this:

'If a man came on the phone to dedicate a record to his wife who was at work, could she say things like, "All on your own, then? I pass your house on my way home, I'll nip in for a cup of tea. Ho, ho."? She could not, she would not. Men can, men do, and women expect them to, even if it's all fantasy. Men in broadcasting are expected to be surrogate lovers, all bold flirtation and innuendo. Women are not. And that . . . is why you'll only ever find us in the earnest corners of radio' (Reynolds, 1979).

This is probably why Aidan Day, Controller of Programmes, Capital Radio, replied when I asked him why he had no female DJs that he would like to have some, but that 'all the women who applied thought they had to talk about nappies all the time' (personal interview). Doreen Davies has also said that she thought a female DJ would alienate women listeners by talking about the housework and making them feel guilty.

'If a girl in some studio in London starts talking about getting your washing and ironing done—you're going to resent it. It just sounds personal to another woman. It's different if Tony Blackburn says it; that's just light-hearted' (Ross, 1977).

The double inference from this is significant: a DJ could not get away *without* mentioning housework; at the same time a DJ who talked about it seriously is unacceptable. It is hard to avoid the conclusion that the strip-shows are music to iron by, chat to etherize the mind—a classic example of palliative radio. They are designed for a specific sub-culture: women who don't go out to paid employment are, in the BBC Audience Research definition of occupational status, 'unoccupied women (most of whom are housewives)' as opposed to 'gainfully occupied women' (BBC Audience Research, 1964).

That housewives are different from the rest of the world was made evident in Capital Radio's franchise application to the IBA:

'In constructing programmes to appeal to women (and to a large extent women as housewives) two things have to be borne in mind . . . Women are sentimental . . . Women are fanatical ... They are escapist, or they are not sufficiently cold-blooded to enjoy drama which, if taken seriously, would represent alarm and despondency. This is what gives them their bias towards stories about hospitals and against stories about guns; towards local issues (where they can see plainly what is at stake) and away from foreign news (of dubious implication); towards happy endings, but happy endings to sagas which are as grittily tough as they know real life usually is' (Capital Radio to the IBA, 1973).

Quite apart from the notion of a grittily tough happy ending, this whole is a masterpiece of doublethink. It categorizes and stereotypes women in the crudest and most traditional way (irrational, extremists, unable to face reality, parochial), but at the same time attempts to soften its impact with approvingly unctuous and apparently flattering alternative explanations.

Almost all the strip-shows share certain fundamental characteristics. Their presenters, like Radio 2's Terry Wogan, have cultivated an air of urbanity—suave, sophisticated, jokey, knowing. They flatter their listeners, they banter with them. The music in between is mostly romantic: Frank Sinatra crooning about love affairs, golden oldies. Radio 2 has developed a deliberately Valium image in its jingles: 'Nice and Easy, Radio 2', 'Easy Listening through the Day'—the emphasis in on nothing disruptive. The DJs make constant reference to their listeners' day: sitting down for a cup of tea, putting your feet up, doing the ironing, etc.—the interaction between romance and domesticity is finely gauged, though for the listeners perhaps frequently bathetic.

From the presenters' comments, a very specific picture of the housewife can be built up: she is young or, at any rate, not old (to Hamilton, 'young at heart'); she is married; she belongs to a nuclear family, with husband (out at work) and children (at school); she does not work outside the home; she does all the housework; she is satisfied at being at home; she is generally content.

David Hamilton asked a housewife, participating in his quiz by phone, how she was managing with kids at home over the summer holidays (August 21, 1979). She took the question a little too seriously, and complained about the extra work and lack of room for them to play. She had obviously ruptured the contented consensual view which is the framework of the programme, and Hamilton did not know how to reply, except to try and find some compensating factor and so restore contentment and reinforce the framework. But the woman continued to complain, and assert her own framework (many, of course, would have given in to the pressure to appear fulfilled). It is hard not to conclude that one of the reasons which excludes women presenters is that they might take such complaints seriously, which could result in the questioning of a whole series of assumptions.

Women, of course, are very important agents of consumption: they control the household budget and so are prime targets for advertisers. A dissonant tone to daytime programming would certainly not be conducive to persuading women to buy, or advertisers to take space, and so must affect the ILR strip shows, and Radios 1 and 2 are in business to compete with them.

Actually, the received wisdom that women would not accept a female DJ has never been tested out by the BBC. The IBA found that 46 per cent of women surveyed thought there were enough women presenting programmes on radio, and 37 per cent thought there were not enough (IBA, 1977). Anne Nightingale, the only BBC female DJ, who broadcasts at weekends, feels that as women avidly read women's magazines and write to them, they would just as readily take to women on the air.

She argues that:

'It's not only women who are listening: you go into a garage to pay, and Radio 1 is on, and not many women work in garages; it's also on in other places of male employment. They've made a demographic error in thinking it's just women listening' (personal interview).

This is true: of listeners to all radio at 9.30–10 a.m. on a weekday when, the producers would have us believe, the men are at work (with the radio off) and the women are at house-work (with the radio on), 12 per cent of all listeners are students, 20 per cent are males working full-time, 11 per cent are females working full-time, 13 per cent are females working part-time, and 36 per cent are housewives. So, although housewives constitute the largest single group, they are by no means the majority. Similarly, at 12–12.30 p.m., though housewives constitute 31 per cent of listeners, there are 14 per cent students, 24 per cent males, and 21 per cent employed females (full and part-time) (personal communication from BBC Audience Research, 1976 figures).

Although this is a profile for all networks, if men are listening at work, they are hardly likely to be listening in their offices to Radio 3 (classical music, middle-aged, middle-class audience)—more likely to Radios 1 and 2 (where there is strip programming) in their factory, shop, or workshop.

It is remarkable how universal the profile of female listeners is in other parts of broad-casting as well. *Afternoon Theatre*, the daily Radio 4 play slot, for example, has well over twice as many female as male listeners. It is usually a pedestrian piece of domestic drama, and it is assumed that its audience needs the world processed into monochrome. 'Themes may be demanding and varied provided the story is easy to follow', according to the BBC's notes to authors (BBC, 1977).

Gilly Fraser, a feminist and playwright who has contributed to the slot, defends it.

'I remember, before I started writing, when I was housebound with four kids and very frustrated, radio in the afternoon saved my life. So what comes out when I write is what it's like to be female—that's conveyed to women in the same state as I was, who'd never go to the theatre. *Afternoon Theatre*, without being polemic, can be truthful about women's lives' (personal interview).

Its new editor, Penny Gold, 28, intends it to be more so.

'I'm anxious to get more of the women who are at home looking after kids or on shift work. They don't get much stimulus because they're stuck at home. I don't think we should talk down to them. I want plays and characters they can empathize with, and about something' (personal interview).

An example is an adaptation of a stage play, *Tissue* by Louise Page. 'It's a kind of evo-cation of what it is about our breasts which makes mastectomy seem so terrible' (personal interview).

Afternoon Theatre is potentially a powerful tool: Micheline Wandor, who has written for it, would like to see it taking a radical, aggressive approach to women's lives. Certainly, radio attracts a large number of women writers, more than other media. One theory is that women are drawn to its personal, private voice. Gilly Fraser thinks it is that women writers are given relatively greater opportunities in radio (personal interview).

The ideology of the nuclear family with its good mother at the centre is prominent in much of the rest of radio directed at women. *Woman's Hour*, though it has initiated open discussion on many contentious subjects, has also neutralized them by its cosy, reassuring tone and even a challenging item tends to be surrounded by bland, traditional topics.

Phone-in and medical advice programmes are an example, where, quite apart from the actual advice, the image of woman-with-a-problem seeking help from man-the-expert (or sometimes woman) is powerfully institutionalized in the very structure. Hilary Graham and Lorna McKee examined ideologies of motherhood and medicine on radio and television (Graham and McKee, 1978). They found that programmes on pregnancy and childbirth tended to emphasize the role of the medical expert, treating the health of the baby as paramount, and the well-being of the pregnant woman as secondary and discounting her desire to take responsibility for her pregnancy. Programmes on parenthood *after* the birth of the baby were, on the other hand, much more oriented to emphasising the mother's responsibility (though under the guidance of paediatricians and child experts).

They also trace some of the common ways in which early infant socialization is shown as an exclusively maternal role—by Wendy Greengross, for example, a frequent radio advice-giver. And by having real-live mothers interviewed on tape and experts situated in the studio answering questions later (a common structure), such radio programmes ensure that mothers never speak *for themselves*, but are always mediated and interpreted by someone else.

They cite a specific example of a phone-in on childbirth, where two experts (both women—a gynaecologist and a health visitor) convey the idea of professional unanimity—for example against home births—and then refer the caller back to her GP, 'an important strategy . . . in ensuring medical hegemony'. A subsequent *Tuesday Call* phone-in on 'Toddlers' (November 30, 1976) with paediatrician Hugh Jolly and child psychologist Penelope Leach is even more revealing.

A woman caller complained about her very active $2\frac{1}{2}$-year-old son, who would not go to bed before midnight. Hugh Jolly's response was to tell the mother that it is not her son's problem, but her problem (implying that she is the problem), and that she should let the child come into her bed. The notion of the good mother as one who makes sacrifices for the good of her child is powerfully inculcated through such a response and such a programme. Phone-ins in general give the illusion of participation in and access to mass media, though, in effect, the level of participation is strictly controlled and, by giving the studio expert or host the final word, they reinforce the unimportance and impotence of the caller.*

It is hard, with such a cluster of examples of status quo radio, to entertain the notion of radio being anything else. But experience elsewhere and, to a very limited extent in this country, has shown otherwise. Numerous alternatives have been tried. In the United States, for example, the idea of feminist radio has typically been diverted into a commercial venture. WOMN–1220 in Connecticut is America's first women's radio station. It is hardly feminist: launched by a man, it provides rich pickings for advertisers, and 'WOMN would avoid at all times a strictly feminist tone' [2]. Nonetheless, they ban what they call 'cock-rock'; at least one in three records is by a female artist, and they have already given exposure to new women performers. They carry 'normal' news, but also emphasize stories about women that other stations might not, like the arrest of a woman breast-feeding her baby in public. Advertisements are screened, and sent back for re-writing if they seem to promote stereotypes of women as helpless or flighty. [3]

---

* Through the social distribution of private telephones in Britain, phone-ins tend to discriminate against the already disenfranchised, those with few opportunities to voice their opinions.

[2] Reported by Ian Ball in *The Daily Telegraph*.

[3] Reported by Fran Hawthorne in *MS Magazine*.

More explicitly sympathetic to feminism is the American National Federation of Community Broadcasters, the body which represents community radio stations. It stipulates that member stations must 'have a stated and demonstrated commitment to the participation of women and Third World people in all aspects of their organization and operations', and delegates from member stations to the NFCB must include either a woman or a Third World person (NFCB, 1978).

Among member stations is KPFA, in Berkeley, California, the oldest listener-sponsored radio station in the world. Karla Tonella, head of Women's Programmes, has deliberately tried to change the relationship between the station's professionals and women's groups who want their campaign or activities aired on KPFA. Offering professional guidance to ease them into acquiring broadcasting skills, she suggests to them that they try and make a programme or item themselves, rather than depend on the professional/subject relationship.

There is a similar attempt to alter the relationship between professional and interviewee in WBAI, the New York station belonging to the same chain (Pacifica) as KPFA. The interviews are markedly different from their BBC equivalent, in which presenters feel constrained to adopt the role of devil's advocate by challenging views offered (especially by feminists) according to some consensual, commonly-held ideology which is never articulated or defined ('some people would say'). The WBAI interviewer is likely to let the interviewee ramble for much longer without the frequent interruptions that her/his BBC colleagues would make. S/he does not feel the need to mediate or interpret the interviewee's position to the audience.

In a WBAI interview on March 3, 1979, two feminists organising a health conference were interviewed by a man. The WBAI interviewer only interjected to clarify, when there was something he didn't understand. He obviously conceived his role as *helping* the women to get their information and opinions across. It wasn't that he had no interpretive framework dictating his questions; rather, it accorded with that of the women. In the BBC, perforce, it would have differed.

The best-known feminist radio station is Radio Donna, in Rome. This is a 2 hour daily opt-out from Radio Città Futura, one of the many Italian private left-wing stations. It is located in San Lorenzo, a working-class district of Rome. Every morning, a group of women would run discussions—often spontaneous phone conversations—on issues hitherto taboo on RAI state radio, such as abortion, wife-battering, etc., and also played women's music. On January 9, 1979, the station was attacked by members of a fascist underground group, NAR (Nuclei Armati Revoluzionarie). Five women were in the studio making a broadcast about abortion and contraception for the 'Housewives Collective' at the time. The attackers set fire to the studio and seriously injured the women. The result was a large demonstration (with 50,000 women) in support of Radio Donna,[4] but the women running the station felt that the men had exploited the attack for their own political ends. The result has been a split, with only the Housewives Collective left participating in the station.[5] Radical feminists have started a new station called Radio Lillith. The Radio Donna experience demonstrates the powerful emotions engendered by feminist radio, and also the difficulties of running feminist radio as part of a mixed station.

British radio has remained remarkably immune from anything but the odd liberal programme. The most unusual and imaginative experiment was a series of programmes

---

[4] From a news report in *The Leveller*, May 1979.
[5] According to an article by Betty Collins in *Women's Voice*.

organized by Radio London, the BBC local radio station, and the Inner London Education Authority, called *Stuck at Home*. It started in 1975 when Sarah Lovegrove, a community development worker, met informally with isolated groups of mothers in the London Borough of Wandsworth for three months. According to producer Keith Yeomans, 'the project was aimed at finding whether local radio could be used to help the self-perceived educational needs of young mothers at home with kids'. As a result of Ms Lovegrove's meetings, the content of the programmes was drawn up by the mothers and herself.

As Sarah Lovegrove explained in her accompanying booklet:

'These programmes were not made with any pre-conceived ideas of my own about what young children *ought* to want. The subject matter has come entirely from conversations I had with many mothers during the summer of 1975' (Lovegrove, 1976).

So Lovegrove's premise, unlike Doreen Davies', is not a prescriptive one, dictating an agenda and framework: she permitted that to be dictated by her listeners, an unusual reversal of roles. She also realized that she must use their domestic lives as the content of the programmes, their centre, and not as background noise against which diverse fantasies could be played out. So that the precise things which Doreen Davies is fighting to keep off the air—a serious consideration of housework, routine, or loneliness, for example—Sarah Lovegrove made into the focus of her series.

The series may have been oriented towards the family (though single parents are referred to in the booklet accompanying the series), but otherwise the programmes indicate the possibilities of presenting another interpretive framework—quite different from the conventional BBC one—which highlights and renders significant different areas of women's lives. There were three series of programmes, on subjects like Getting Depressed, Getting Angry with the Children, Feeling Lonely, A Mum's Job, Making Time for Yourself, Getting Out into the Community, etc. Many of the programmes were listened to by mothers in groups and used as the basis for discussion.

Sarah Lovegrove continued: .

'As you will see, the programmes were not just opportunities for mothers to say what they felt. Other mothers, whose children are now older, listened to the problems and offered listeners their own personal solutions. So in the first series of programmes there are no "experts", no professionals telling women what to do, and how to cope. Rather there is a sharing of common problems and experiences' (Lovegrove, 1976).

Compare this with the ideology of phone-ins, and especially *Tuesday Call's* 'Toddlers' programme, with its experts/ordinary mothers division, and its typecasting of women in the role of people-with-problems. Here, women are those with solutions as well.

Finally, Lovegrove notes that:

'You may notice that there is very little in any of the programmes for or about the children. This is not an omission but rather a conscious choice to hear about the needs of mothers as people rather than as mothers' (Lovegrove, 1976).

Again, this is an explicit contrast with the ideologies which Graham and McKee discovered, where women *qua* women were secondary to their all-important role as mother. It is also markedly at variance with Hugh Jolly's approach.

Although a single series *Stuck at Home* shows some of the alternative possibilities in their existing organization. Another new project taking advantage of established stations is being run by Jane Thompson, a lecturer at the University of Southampton, who will be running a series on Radio Solent next spring to 'teach the basics of politics to working-class women in a stimulating and entertaining way' (EOC, 1979). Thompson has already run a similar project last summer with the ILR station Radio Victory: the series *Think for Yourself* resulted in two study groups in Portsmouth and Southampton which discussed issues around 'Women's rights and wrongs' raised by one of the programmes.

She has received a £2000 grant from the Equal Opportunities Commission for the new project. The series will use interviews, phone-ins, and studio discussion, as well as performances by a community theatre group, to interest women in British politics at neighbourhood, local, and national level. The series will be followed up by an off-air advisory service, and study groups on housing-estates, in womens' groups, etc.

Jane Thompson believes:

'We have to exercise positive discrimination to women in general but particularly to working-class women whose education and job opportunities are most restricted. The circumstances they come across in their everyday lives, like working in low-paid jobs and hassles with the social security, means they are aware of their own difficulties but they don't realize these things can be altered. If you can get groups of working-class women together to realize that these are not personal problems but political problems, they will develop an understanding that they can do something about it rather than just accepting it as a fact of life' (EOC, 1979).

Evidently, a wholly different framework from that employed by David Hamilton.

Women's Radio Workshop is an entirely new group which also seeks, in the first instance, to have its programmes broadcast in existing stations, after they have been independently made. It was formed in March 1979 after a workshop on women and radio at the Socialist-Feminist Conference in London, where 35–40 women discussed issues on feminist radio and played tapes. The Workshop is open to women only, and almost none of its members are professional broadcasters.

Among its aims is 'to promote radio programmes made for and by women, which will give a clearer understanding of the position of women in society and seek means of changing it'. A further aim explicitly seeks to challenge the conventional broadcasting divisions—'to make programmes in which the usual barrier of "professionalism" between producer and subject is broken down so that those who participate in programmes can work with WRW and have more control over content and presentation' (List of Aims, WRW, 1979).

The group is starting by making programmes to offer to existing local radio stations, and would like to acquire regular broadcast time on these stations, so that through their large audiences women's views which are rarely heard in the media will reach women including those who do not identify with the women's movement. The group is completing work on its first two programmes: one is on women's music, a documentary about women playing accoustic music, talking about the relationship between performer and audience, sharing skills, commercialism, interspersed with their songs and music; the other is on AID—Artificial Insemination by Donor—including discussions with lesbian women who have done AID without medical help. Cassettes and leaflets accompany the programmes, for the non-broadcast back-up to the programmes is considered an essential feature. It is hoped that the listeners might listen in groups, and not only alone, and will discuss and perhaps act upon the programme thus changing the relationship between broadcaster and listener, so that the listener is not simply a passive consumer of a transient product.

Both these programmes take areas of women's culture and experience usually avoided by radio, and try to discuss them in a sympathetic but accessible way. Groups like this focus on the question of whether feminists should be trying to slot into existing mass media—with mass exposure and all the compromises this entails—or trying to create their own women-originated forms and outlets. Although ultimately the latter would obviously give a far greater measure of control, it might preclude non-feminists finding such programmes by chance and might also justify the further neglect of women's issues by other radio stations. WRW has decided to concentrate on established radio stations for the time being.

At present with a new Conservative government in Britain, it seems likely that commercial radio will flourish at the expense of public service broadcasting. This will exacerbate the tendency to treat women as housewife/consumers. To counter this, women must fight on a variety of fronts. They must join the campaign for a more pluralistic system of radio in Britain, which would enable women to develop their own stations and broadcasting forms, as well as to participate in existing and forthcoming ones. They must play a prominent role in the debate about 'access' since women who are not professional broadcasters are doubly disenfranchised from access to the airwaves. And they must constantly explicate the hidden framework which underpins most radio programmes for and about women, so that oppressive inferences are openly condemned by women.

ADDENDUM

Since the above was written, two significant developments have taken place:

(1) The Women's Radio Workshop has extended its analysis of women and radio in a grant application to the Arts Council. They said:

'An average day's listening to Radio 4 . . . leaves the woman listener convinced that her concerns are getting her family through breakfast cheerfully (*Today*), politics have nothing to do with her (*The News*), Christianity is the cultural norm (*The Daily Service*), men are cleverer than women (*My Word*), her creativity is limited to domestic skills (*Woman's Hour*), her children are her own and no-one else's responsibility (*Listen with Mother*), and that other women's lives are slightly more glamourous than her own (*The Archers/Afternoon Theatre*).'

As well as attempting to find women engineers in radio—and failing to find more than one—the WRW is clarifying its vision of an alternative relationship between women and radio:

'Since radio communicates largely through language, it is important to understand the potential for change in our ideas that exists when, for instance, we are involved in a discussion for recording; when we talk something through, it's possible to shift our perception of the world. We see programme-making as a process in which we're not only developing our technical skills, but also affecting our lives. . . . Many women have remarked, on first learning how to edit, that it gives them a clearer understanding of the power of the media—splicing a tape with a razor blade is a simple enough operation, but it has enormous consequences. By working with women in making our own tapes, we are grasping some of that power for ourselves. Developing interview techniques which enable a creative use of language and an equality of participation, for the interviewees is an important part of our work' (WRW, Arts Council grant application, 1979).

(2) The first Feminist Radio Network conference was held in Washington DC in September 1979. Carys Pearce of the WRW attended, and I am grateful to her for the following information. The Network is committed to educating and informing the public about women via radio and audio tapes. They want women to be able to speak directly to the audience in their own style, and aim to make their programmes non-rhetorical, entertaining, and thought-provoking. They want their current affairs programmes to 'stimulate the listener to an awareness of the possibilities for her own life, and encourage her own thinking and participation' (*FRN Catalog*, 1979).

The conference was attended by 150 women working in public service broadcasting, university radio, the Pacifica chain, and commercial stations, from all over the United States and even Alaska. The conference, as well as putting women in touch with each other, sought to encourage women to get paid for the work they do in radio stations, often on a voluntary basis. The women who attended did all kinds of jobs in radio, from engineer to Director of News. The conference was very committed to sharing information and demystifying radio, and there was a lot of technical equipment to try out.

One of the women who attended presents and engineers her own hour-long show (*The Velvet Sledge-hammer*) on a New York station once a fortnight entirely single-handed, without an engineer in the studio! Many of the women at the conference worked on their own in stations rather than in women's collectives. Some women were trying to take a feminist perspective on news, by focussing on women's issues, such as a lesbian march on Washington, and discussing how to get away from sensationalist reporting.

Carys Pearce concluded that 'the tapes I heard were wonderful—a creative and imaginative use of sound. They were women who saw making radio programmes as an art-form, experimentally; they were not concerned in any way with the question of objectivity' (personal interview). The Network distributes feminist radio programmes on subjects ranging from battered wives, office workers, waitresses, poor women and the economy, to the arts (women's fiction, poetry, etc.).

REFERENCES

Annan. 1977. Report of the committee on the future of broadcasting. HMSO, London.

Ball, Ian. January 1979. When women take over the airwaves. *The Daily Telegraph*, London.

BBC Audience Research. 1964. Sound drama audiences. BBC, London.

BBC. 1977. Notes on Radio Drama. BBC, Radio Drama Script Unit, London.

Capital Radio, 1973. Capital Radio Programme Plans, IBA. London.

Collins, Betty. February 1979. Rome women face fascist attacks. *Women's Voice*, London.

Community Communications Group. 1977. Comments on the recommendations of the Annan Committee on the future of broadcasting. ComCom., London.

EOC. August 1979. University in 3-way link-up. EOC News.

Graham and McKee. 1978. Ideologies of motherhood and medicine on radio and television. Institute of Social and Economic Research, University of York.

Hawthorne, Fran. March 1979. Tuning in on the voice of WOMN-AM. *MS*,.

IBA. 1977. The need for speech: a study of listeners' attitudes. IBA, London.

The Leveller. May 1979. Future City Hit. London.

Lewis, Peter, M. 1978. Whose media? The Annan report and after: a citizen's guide to radio and television. Consumer's Association, London.

Lovegrove, Sarah. 1976. Stuck at home. Bethnal Green Institute of Adult Education, London.

NFCB. 1978. Annual Report. NFCB. Washington.

Reynolds, Gillian. February 19th 1979. Women's Place, Broadcast, London.

Rodger, Ian. August 9th 1979. The box, *New Society*. IPC, London.

Ross, Mileva. 1977. *Is This Your Life? Images of Women in the Media*. King, Josephine and Stott, Mary, eds. Virago, London.

Singer, Aubrey. August 1979. Radio and the eighties: art and writing. BBC.

Wandor, Micheline. 1978. *Tales I Tell my Mother*. Journeyman Press, London.

Women's Studies Int. Quart., 1980, Vol. 3, pp. 55–57
© Pergamon Press Ltd.   Printed in Great Britain

0148–0685/80/0301–0055/$02.00/0

FEMINIST ART PRACTICE AND THE MASS MEDIA: A 'PERSONAL' ACCOUNT

PEN DALTON

31 Park Street, Brighton BN2 2BN, U.K.

(*Accepted August* 1979)]

Like many other women artists, my skills and preferences lie in the direction of textiles, painting and drawing. Being the mother of two small children these art practices have been so much easier, in a practical sense, to organize around housework and a part-time job.

At art school I trained in painting, fabric printing and embroidery. Nobody forced me into these 'feminine' areas; it seemed to me at the time that I had followed my own talents and exercised my own free will in opting for textiles and painting. I was aware, of course, that there were no men in the textile department and only a few doing life drawing. In the painting studios, whilst I painted small, they were all engaged on huge abstract canvases. While women practised 'traditional' methods of sculpture, the men did welding and plastics. At this time (in the sixties) the newly introduced screen-printing, photography and film media were almost totally the concern of men.

Huge paintings and sculpture have now been abandoned by the sharp male art student, who is now 'into' video, film and TV. As we feminists begin to collect together our hidden drawings and paintings and are struggling to get our work validated in art galleries male artists are moving away from the gallery system into film production, photography and mass communications. Whatever is the dominant art practice, is taken over by men.

Nonetheless, feminist artists are now succeeding in using traditional women's arts, such as knitting and sewing, so that in many cases it has become part of a new *avant-garde* and we are now witnessing a new male interest in formerly despised 'women's work'; not so much in sympathy with feminist issues as a desire to keep up with the latest 'feminist scene'.[1]

What I think is dangerous is that feminist art will be taken over by the male-dominated art institutions and placed into a linear 'Art History' context, labelled as another 'ism' to follow Surrealism and Modernism. It faces the danger of being absorbed and neutralized into the monolithic Art Industry. We already experience the way in which feminist issues become new fodder to sell products and distort our intended meanings: 'Liberator' washing machines. At the same time as we demand recognition and equal participation as artists, we are conscious of the situation in the United States where feminism is a big new source of selling power and the women's movement seems to be able to do little about it.

What seems to me to be important to feminist art practice, is what happens to our images and representations once they have left our control. For their final meanings depend upon the context in which they appear.

What concerns me is that the vast majority of women, housewives, factory and office workers, do not visit art galleries or have access to feminist literature through existing

---

[1] See, for example, Lawrence Alloway, Women's art in the 70s. *Art in America.*

distribution processes. Even with shows and events in libraries, shopping centres and parks, most women get their ideas about art/feminism/femininity through the mass media—TV, film, women's magazines. As artists and feminists, we only have male-controlled selection procedures and filters through which to disseminate our ideas on a large scale.

The showing of the 'Feministo Event'[2] at the ICA was a terrific move. It took our private practices in art and domestic work into the public sphere of 'Art' and so raised questions about the nature of art, of women's work and femininity. Similarly, the placing of Tricia Davies' and Phil Goodall's 'Mother's Pride, Mothers' Ruin'[3] into academic conferences brought to the fore many questions about the content and form of academic research, the presentation of findings, and the primacy of the written word in research. Mary Kelly's 'Post Partum Document'[4] posed many of the above questions in taking what is usually considered private and personal—Motherhood—and putting it into a 'legitimate' academic context.

But the 'Feministo Event' reached the mass of women only via the press; 'Mother's Pride, Mother's Ruin' has reached mainly academic and feminist audiences. Mary Kelly's 'Post Partum Document', although respected amongst *avant-garde* artists, was trivialized by the press.

Being a feminist artist is problematic. Through our education system girls are 'encouraged' to prefer those school subjects in the arts and humanities which can only lead to positions of less economic power and control in society: they are also 'encouraged' to specialize in yet further less prestigious and powerless areas. I can see that while I have regarded my preference for textiles and life drawing as a personal choice of a medium of expression, it has many—convenient—repercussions for I have in fact circumscribed my own influence; textiles and life drawing are not the medium for reaching mass audiences. Within this area I am able to construct representations but once again it is males who have the power to juxtapose and manipulate the final meanings which are then disseminated through television, film and photograph. But it is not a satisfactory resolution of this problem to simply devalue those areas which have been traditionally associated with women, which enjoy low prestige, which reach only a limited audience in their original form, and which offer few opportunities for power and control.

Knitting and embroidery, as we know can be used just as well as any other media to present feminist ideas and values; they are not inherently feminine media but have become associated with females and perhaps because of this, unlike photography and film, do not have the same financial resources made available to them for their production and distribution. My painting in a gallery for instance, which could represent a critique of the existing images of women, will be seen by only a few; trite advertisements which perpetuate non-feminist images are seen by millions on hoardings and in women's magazines.

As an art teacher I may be able to shift the emphasis of my teaching from drawing and painting and 'girl's crafts' to teaching about representations and the mass media, not because I think that these are the 'correct' media for feminist artists but because I think girls should be aware of the contribution which the media make to the construction of femininity. If girls still do *choose* the traditionally feminine media, at least it will be a choice made from an understanding of the implications that are involved.

---

[2] The 'Feministo Postal Event' began as women posted art works to each other as private communication. It was shown at the Institute for Contemporary Arts in London (June 1977).

[3] 'Mother's Pride, Mother's Ruin' was first shown at a British Sociological Association annual conference.

[4] Mary Kelly's Post Partum Document, 1976 at the ICA, The Museum of Modern Art, Oxford (1977).

To make this change as a teacher I have had to learn new skills and re-evaluate my art practice. For some time now, for example, I have been making posters which, although technically inferior to my paintings, are at least bought and seen and do not remain in a pile under the bed.

As an individual I can do little to interrupt the vast communications networks but at school, I can introduce new evaluations and questions; I can at least present girls with the option of entering what have been almost exclusively male areas and I can encourage them to re-evaluate the 'traditional' women's media. So many girls readily accept embroidery and fabric printing as 'naturally' feminine and neither question this classification (and its implications) nor entertain the possibility of entering media work.

Perhaps it is not simply a question of whether to continue to work within the female tradition with the disadvantages that brings, nor to abandon that female tradition; perhaps girls should be presented with the option of entering both areas. Such a strategy would certainly be an improvement on the unthinking channelling of females and males which has too frequently been passed off as 'natural inclination'. Ideally, this could lead to a re-evaluation of the traditional feminine areas and an infiltration of women into the areas which exercise control.

Feminist artists working in the mass media could provide the women's movement with some access to control; they could also help to subvert and interrupt existing media practices. (When women have access to these resources they could also be instrumental in according greater prestige to the traditional feminine areas and obtain the benefits that accompany such a classification.) Currently, women have neither the power nor the money to create alternative systems which could reach millions of people in the way that existing mass communications do, nor is it desirable that we should do so. The search for a 'true' or 'essential' feminist art practice could be self-defeating; we need to use what we have and to appropriate what we want.

Women's Studies Int. Quart., 1980, Vol. 3, pp. 59–61
Pergamon Press Ltd. Printed in Great Britain

CAMERAWOMAN OBSCURA:
A 'PERSONAL' ACCOUNT*

DIANE TAMMES

9 Queen's Drive, London, N4, U.K.

(*Accepted November* 1979)

'I want to do it because I want to do it. Women must try to do things men have tried. When they fail, their failure must be but a challenge to others.' (Amelia Earhart).

I would encourage more women to think of themselves as technicians.

In 1975 I was one of the first camerawomen to be accepted by the Association of Cinematograph Television and Allied Technicians (ACTT). Since then I have been working as a camerawoman in both film and television.[1] It is difficult to analyse one's position as a woman technician in the industry as a whole; it is perhaps easier to think about women as a minority group in the technical grades.

In 1979 there are approximately four camerawomen, two women sound recordists, four women sound assistants and twelve women camera assistants working within the ACTT. There are at present two main ways of admission to the ACTT open to women: they can either follow a course at one of the recognized film schools (The National Film School, The Royal College of Art, The London Polytechnic) or they can be taken on as an assistant in a film company which will guarantee to employ them for 2 years and then apply to go on the employment list.

Other women work independently outside the union through choice or lack of the necessary training.

I began my own career in 1963 as a freelance still photographer in Edinburgh. The sixties was a very rich and productive time for the theatre, improvised theatre, travelling companies and new ways of writing and presenting plays. I photographed publicity material for the

---

* I would like to thank Helen Baehr who turned my efforts to write about my work into more readable prose.

[1] Since 1975 I have worked on approximately 30 films including:

1975: *Adam* a documentary financed by Medical Grant (camera).
1976: *Some Women of Marrakech* a documentary for Granada TV (camera).
1976: *Riddles of the Sphinx* a film financed by British Film Institute (lighting camerawoman).
1977: *Rapunzel Let Down your Hair* a film financed by British Film Institute (lighting camerawoman).
1978: *Angel in the House* a film financed by British Film Institute (lighting camerawoman).
1978: *Communist Party* a documentary for Granada TV (camera).
1978: *One Fine Day* a drama for London Weekend TV (focus puller and second camera).
1979: *Only a Game* a drama for Thames TV (focus puller).
1979: *Sandra and Louise* (working title) a feature film for Kestrel Films (focus puller).
1979: *Fats and Figures* a documentary for BBC TV (camera).
1979: *Division* a film financed by British Film Institute (lighting camerawoman).
1979: *Women* a documentary for Thames TV (camera).

theatre, attended rehearsals and used the existing set lighting and effects. By living and working in the same space I could combine studio and dark-room work with looking after my child. I enjoyed the solitude of working as a photographer, the pressure of producing on time and capturing single images. I did not analyse my work and accepted that the images I made were my own images.

This experience in the theatre and my work in portraiture, photographics and photo-journalism formed a sound basis for much of my subsequent work in film. In 1972 I applied to the postgraduate course in film offered by the National Film School. At that time the course took 3 years and was unstructured which meant that you were given a budget, equipment and facilities and told to 'get on with it'. The lack of structure seemed limitless. I tried to limit myself. I wanted to look at the work of camera*men*, to examine the techniques they used, their camera movements and lighting skills. I shot and lit as many films as possible during those 3 years. I made my own short films and tried my hand at editing and sound recording. I watched films, discussed them collectively and worked to evolve some critique in my own mind of their worth.

This experience contrasted strongly to the time I had spent working as a photographer to my own time scale on my own. I found the medium of film challenging and difficult. Most ways for women seemed completely blocked. Tutors were drawn from the film industry which provided direct access to the medium but also a back-up of 'ways of doing things' which could be restrictive. We were swamped with the films already produced by a male-dominated film industry. There were no women on the staff. Out of 75 students at the Film School only 11 were women.

The cameras Elair NPR, Arriflex, Aaton, filters, lenses and intricacies of the matt box seemed strange and unwieldy at first. I felt my struggles with the equipment were very public. I felt too closely observed for comfort. It took a long time to acquire the dexterity to be unselfconscious. But once learnt the technical mystique became a tool to be used. The hardest task of all was just to feel that I was talented and courageous enough to persist. My self-doubts and struggle to break new ground often made me seem too radical and I was regarded with suspicion and hostility. The National Film School had negotiated an arrangement with the ACTT and I obtained my ticket when I left in 1975.

Working in a film industry which is occupied almost totally by men and into which women are seen as an intrusion is difficult. Energy goes primarily into creating the best possible impression and being impossibly perfect. As women technicians we are challenging a traditionally male occupation and the position held for too long that women cannot cope with technical jobs.

I am often the only woman on a technical crew and it is my responsibility as a camera-woman to lead the crew of sound recordist, sound assistant, camera assistant and electrician. When I arrive on location with a male assistant *he* is approached as the cameraperson. There is a belief commonly held by male technicians that if a woman can do the job it is not worth doing. A camera*man* is seen as a macho technical expert and this notion supports the egos of some directors. It is difficult for them to accept a woman behind the camera because it demeans their position.

Independent film-makers are becoming more accustomed to women technicians and as more of us acquire the necessary skills we are beginning to see that women are producing essentially different and exciting films of their own. Women working within the television industry are joining in the struggle to use freelance all-women crews where they see the need, since there are insufficient numbers of women technicians on the staff of TV companies. As an experienced camerawoman, however, I am still not accepted by the feature film industry where my role so far has been as a focus puller or second camera operator.

The only way that the number of women technicians will increase is if we create more space within the system for ourselves. We need to petition for training schemes and positive discrimination programmes for women at all the technical levels. We must work on every kind of film and not allow ourselves to be ghettoized into restricted areas producing only films for women about women.

New opportunities are opening for us, can be opened by us. I would encourage more women to think of themselves as technicians for the skills are not difficult to acquire. The idea that women who do something different are 'exceptional' is not true: I am doing something I have been trained to do and that training must be opened to more women.

'As women recognise their strengths and as they raise their own concerns, they can, not only progress towards a new synthesis, but simultaneously clarify and make more obvious the issue central to all human beings.'[2]

Women's technical skills, their creativity and imagination are something different and more than just a synthesis of all that men have achieved so far.

---

[2] Miller, Jean Baker. 1976. *Towards a New Psychology of Women*. Pelican, Harmondsworth.

Women's Studies Int. Quart., 1980, Vol. 3, pp. 63–78
Pergamon Press Ltd. Printed in Great Britain

'THE ADVICE OF A REAL FRIEND.'
CODES OF INTIMACY AND OPPRESSION IN WOMEN'S MAGAZINES 1937–1955

Joy Leman

38 The Chase, London SW4, U.K.

(*Accepted November* 1979)

Synopsis—A code of intimacy is inscribed in the language of women's magazines which seems intended to set up a 'sisterly' relationship between magazine and reader.

This paper sets out to study the way in which women are constructed in the text of women's magazines in Britain in the period spanning the late 1930s to the early 1950s. The image of the working woman is foregrounded throughout this time, but in a way which—particularly during the Second World War—indicates the shaping presence of economic and ideological determinants which usually remain invisible in the media product.

1. 'THE ADVICE OF A REAL FRIEND'

'Do you know, I like to think that *Woman's Own* is rather like one of those friends we specially value, the ones who are always the same and always different.' (*Woman's Own*, 11 September 1937).

'Write to me in greater detail about your lost love affairs, your feelings, your conversations.' (*Woman*, 1939).

'This is your page as well as ours—the page we meet to exchange views, ideas, information. Whatever you have to say, why not say it here? We'll have an answer for you.' (*Woman*, 1939).

'Never before have there been such opportunities for women in engineering, but its up to you. Give the men a surprise by proving that even the more skilled jobs are not beyond you.' (*Woman*, December 11, 1943).

These comments addressed to the readership could have appeared in almost any issue of mass circulation women's magazines during the past four decades. The direct address, commanding both intimacy and identification still constitutes the principal tone of women's magazines in Britain. The significance of this tone of intimacy and confidentiality is that it attempts to establish some kind of 'sisterly' relationship between magazine and reader. It tries to locate and exploit the isolated and fragmented position of women in the family, as part of domestic production and as part of the resource pool of labour outside the home, both of which are required by capitalism to maintain itself.

Women are not addressed in the magazines as workers, or as voters, or as tenants, even though many women during the past half century have been all these. The level of communication is personal, individual, a bridge into what Zaretsky (1976) calls 'personal life under capitalism'—a carefully structured no-go area in terms of political ideas or perspectives of change in society. The 'personal' is of course political in that those areas of life—the family, sexuality, sexual relationships—privatized by the particular needs of capitalism at given historical periods are at present an integral part of the political and economic structure of capitalism. The discourse of intimacy adopted by women's magazines denies the existence of this structure.

In trying to understand the way the code of intimacy is intended to operate in the text, it is useful to consider an approach to textual analysis developed in film theory. This involves the notion of a hierarchy of discourse which in the novel 'privileges' the 'voice' of the novelist over reported dialogue, authenticating it as the reader's view of the world (McCabe, 1974; Johnston, 1975). Similarly, in the woman's magazine it seems to me that direct address is used to privilege editorial assumptions about the reader's view of herself.

'Are you worried? Would you like the advice of a real friend? Are you anxious to know what the future holds for you? If so tell your troubles to Madam Sunya.'

This subheading appears in the astrology column of an issue of *Peg's Paper* in 1938 beneath the title 'Let the stars solve your problems'. The suggestion that a mystical solution can somehow deal with readers' troubles fits in with the overall assumption of the magazines that woman should maintain an expressive spiritual role as well as that of practical home-maker. The likely problems facing the readership—bad housing, unemployment, battering by husbands—were not the ones usually recognized by the magazines. Editorial objectives during the period covered indicate a shaping of the magazine based on both these assumptions. Mary Grieves (1964) and James Drawbell (1968) at one time editors of two major women's magazines, admit that an important objective was the identification of the magazine as an individual mentor in the mind of the reader, a source of personal support and problem solving.

The success or failure of such objectives is clearly difficult to prove in any conclusive way as with many other areas of audience and readership response. Circulation figures do not necessarily indicate *how* we 'read' newspapers and magazines, any more than viewing figures indicate *how* we 'read'/interpret/decode a television programme. The significant factor is that the editors seem to have had complete confidence in the possibility of achieving their objectives as well as complete confidence in their definition of women's location in society.

The presentation of women in the media is often structured as 'neutral' description, as if no element of mediation is involved. What is intended to appear as a seamless garment of neutrality, carefully conceals the work of construction of the media product. But this is an essential aspect of the ideology of capitalism, and in particular of the ideology of the media—that their operations are rendered invisible. The processes of production, the conventions of the genre, the industrial practices, the training of personnel, the organizational and financial structures are hidden from view.

Most women are wives and mothers and largely trained for and engaged in domestic production, therefore, the argument goes, it is somehow 'natural' that magazines aimed at a readership of women should 'reflect'[1] this fact and service these 'feminine interests', adopting a suitable expressive tone to do so. The links with advertisers and the benefits to them of this shaping of 'femininity' are not referred to. The benefit to the State of a continually

---

[1] The assertion that the material of women's magazines 'mirrors the attitudes of the readers' is made by Richard Hoggart in '*The Uses of Literacy*' published in 1958. Raymond Williams '*Communications*' (1962) makes a valuable but isolated contribution by stressing the materiality of the magazine as manufactured product. He also notes 'the exclusion from most of these magazines of all references to public affairs. The non-political world which this exclusion creates is not without its clear social vales, of consumption, personal competition and social success.'

available pool of labour, unorganized, unconfident, and simultaneously nurturing the next generation of workers, is not referred to. Instead, the incantations of false intimacy are foregrounded—a discourse of friendliness, reassuring and relocating women in an identity of oppression and a position of exploitation.

'A woman's magazine can get nearer to a woman than her husband or her doctor can.'

This comment was made by James Drawbell, an editor of *Woman's Own* just after the Second World War (Drawbell, 1968). His autobiography describes the magazine then as providing a response to 'the eternal feminine yearning' which he says arises for women during 'the lonely hours of shopping and domestic chores . . . which leave her time for the inner thoughts, the deep longings, the dream of life she would like to live'. Drawbell saw women as lonely and dependent: 'This dependence calling for affection and companionship makes a woman painfully vulnerable'. Drawbell's patriarchal assumptions have the biographer's gloss of romanticism. A more overtly hard-headed commercial approach to the woman reader as consumer is expressed, in her autobiography, by the editor of *Woman* magazine from 1940 to 1962:

'At a very early age women begin their lifelong concern with the market place. A teenage girl will have matriculated in her study of clothes and cosmetics and be ready and willing to embrace the whole field of furnishings and home making durable goods with her engagement ring. Because the magazines go with her all the way in this preoccupation with her personal responsibility for spending the family income, it is essential that they should convince her of their paramount authority . . . . The confidence in the magazines which is engendered in the readers is a big part of the profitability to advertisers.' (Grieves, 1964).

The editorial policy and level of discourse of women's magazines during this twenty-year period, and almost certainly beyond—continuing in the present publications—seems to indicate attempts to locate and exploit the position of women as readership subjects framed within what was considered by the producers of the magazines to be a 'feminine' mode of communications—one dealing with and in the 'personal', the emotions.

The magazines in this study include *Woman, Woman's Own, Woman's Friend, Home Chat, Peg's Paper*. I read a total of 60 issues of these magazines, covering the period of the late 1930s to the early 1950s. This period of the magazines seems particularly useful to analyse because of the alterations made in crucial factors of production, largely due to the determining factor of the war.

The commercial/advertising pressures on the magazines which were just beginning in the late 1930s were suddenly replaced in the war years with a more explicit intervention by the State and the use of the magazines as vehicles for government information and propaganda. Simultaneously the need for more women in the industrial labour force posed potentially contradictory demands on women's magazines. Could the conventions within which they were set up—with their principal focus on the home, motherhood, women's appearance—encompass the image of women involved in 'men's work' in heavy industry and even encourage women to take up this work? The extent to which the magazines were able to adapt to this 'new' image of women and still retain their basic character in terms of the ideology of femininity perhaps indicates how far women's magazines as a genre are defined by an attitude to women which is fundamentally oppressive, and caught within the dominant discourse of capitalist society.

2. MYTHOLOGY IN THE MAGAZINES

As media products women's magazines are part of an ideological apparatus presenting a view of the world which is at most points locked into the economic and political interests of the capitalist system.

At control and production levels the apparatus consists of layers of editors, advertising managers, company directors, newspaper owners, financial backers of various kinds, government advisors and ministers, who tend to share a common view, not only of how society in general should be organized, but in particular, of the place of women within it. This interlocking of financial interests, State control, and media producers might be difficult to demonstrate as a 'power elite',[2] and unnecessary to expose as a conscious conspiracy.

The defining concept of what constitutes a 'woman's magazine' may have evolved over 200 years, in response to the needs and developments of the system (White, 1970). However, the conventions which make up that definition of the genre at the level of presentation and content—inclusion of household advice, questions of childcare, fashion, fiction, letters page, advertising—fix the parameters of the publication. A set of professional routines is established which are seen as essential, defining characteristics 'inherited' and operated by those involved directly in the production of the magazines. The routines are assumed as 'givens' in terms of journalistic practice, constituting the very fabric of 'woman's magazine' and are rarely acknowledged as the bearers of a particular value system. Decisions made or inherited by those in the front line of production of the magazine are unlikely to challenge the defining conventions which shape the product and structure its ideological message. This extends to selection of subject areas, division of subject areas into the categories of the magazine, prioritization of material according to layout, style of writing, use of illustration, cartoon, photography and the associated codes of composition, colour, juxtaposition with text and advertising material—all of which make up the encoded discourse of the magazine, presenting a particular view of the world.

The static format of the magazines is often 'read off' as reflecting the exclusive interests of women. That easy equation 'naturalizes' and feeds into oppressive myths of femininity. Barthes' notion of myth (deriving from Marx) is useful in identifying this process in which cultural/media phenomena are rendered 'natural' in appearance:

'Myth consists in overturning culture into nature or at least the social, the cultural, the ideological, the historical into the "natural". What is nothing but a product of class division and its moral, cultural, and aesthetic consequences is presented (stated) as being a "matter of course"; under the effect of mythical inversion, the quite contingent foundations of the utterance become Common Sense, Right Reason, the Norm, General Opinion' (Barthes, 1977).

'Women interests' as defined in the magazines are naturalized and ghettoized, although of course in a wider social context they are also 'inferiorized' by being *women's* interests.

One of the contradictions of the magazines is that they often begin to define the problems of women in a partial sense. Fundamental questions regarding wage levels, Trade Union

---

[2] C. Wright Mills's theory of the 'power elite' could well apply here even before the days of takeovers and ownership amalgamations. A further study would have to be made to draw out the rather imperceptible, but ultimately significant, supportive contacts between powerful individuals in media, government, industry, finance, etc. at business lunches, receptions, directors' meetings, or even on open-day, visiting their children at prep/public school. It is as much a cementing of values, a common philosophy/view of the world which is involved, as the directive over editorial policy or advertizing links and financial controls.

organization, how to deal with bad landlords, how to form a Tenants Association, how to deal with violent husbands/boyfriends/fathers, are generally excluded. Recent issues of women's magazines have raised these questions, including abortion, sometimes in 'sympathetic' terms but rarely presenting real solutions. The format of the magazine remains the same with covers of cosmetic smiles, significations of seasonal optimism—Christmas holly, Autumn leaves, Spring blossom—endlessly recuperating and trivializing the rare occasions when the stark practicalities of women's oppression are introduced into the magazines.

Janice Winship (1978) discusses how women's magazines in the 1970s 'recognise the problem of femininity, yet finally refuse it as a problem. . . . Our femininity is not something any of us can escape. All of us as women "achieve" our subjectivity in relation to a definition of women which is in part propounded by women's magazines.'

The eternal Catch-22 of the woman's magazine is that, in Marjorie Ferguson's words, it is part of a 'gender-genre' (Ferguson, 1978). It pursues a 'policy of purdah' and will by definition refuse to bring into question the values/ideology by which it achieves its position both in the media and within a gender culture which is central to the reproduction of the ideology of femininity. The interface of economic and ideological determinants is foregrounded in the commercial/cultural context and discourse of the magazines.

The production of the magazine for profit is a structural determinant on the magazine as ideological discourse. Advertising constitutes a major element at both levels and was an important feature during the period dealt with in the study, as much for its reduced quantity and different emphasis in the war period as for its gradual expansion prior to the war, and consolidation of commercial links with the magazine after the war.

3. PRE-WAR: WHITE COLLAR WIVES AND WORKERS—A GUIDE TO BEHAVIOUR. 'IF YOU LOOKED LIKE A FOUR ALE GIRL YOU WOULDN'T GET THE JOB'

The end of the 1930s marked the beginning of the large scale expansion of women's magazines[3] and consolidation of the links with advertisers which was continued and extended after the derestriction of wartime control of newsprint and with the start of post-war economic expansion generally.

In carrying out a textual analysis of issues of *Woman, Woman's Own, Woman's Friend, Home Chat* and *Peg's Paper* published in 1938, I found an unexpected consistency of theme and imagery. In particular the image of the working woman is stressed repeatedly, both in the advertising material and in fiction and feature articles. The work presented is usually, but not always, white collar—shop assistants and secretaries recur most often—and the image of the working woman does not always signal approval.

This is indicated in the following, fairly typical example of professional, career woman image. The drawing of the woman dominates the back cover of *Woman's Friend* with an advert for breakfast cereal. The caption anchors the image in a way that undercuts approval

---

[3] The magazine *Woman* had established a substantial mainly middle-class readership with a circulation figure of 0·75 million by 1940 after 3 years of publication. Most of the pre-war surveys of readership were 'unofficial' (unaudited). A survey carried out in 1939 by the Incorporated Practitioners in Advertizing showed that *Woman* magazine readers were mostly spread across Social Classes B and C, whilst *Woman's Own* readers were mainly in Social Class C. There appear to be no readership figures available during wartime but it seems likely that a rapid increase in readership in all social classes took place in those 5 years and that sales figures or print runs do not represent the number of readers. That is, the magazines were passed around endlessly, probably till they fell apart.

Fig. 1. *Woman's Friend*, 19 March 1938.

of 'career woman'. The figure, dressed in a suit, but with soft 'pussy cat' tie at the neck (signifying femininity) is shown operating two separate pieces of equipment—typewriter and telephone. This is unusual as a media depiction of a woman, but the caption comments on her from its privileged position that she may be 'A source of ceaseless energy . . . but there's danger in this grinding activity—a danger to health and beauty. That's why she should be careful to watch—the five food values in Shredded Wheat' (*Woman's Friend*, March 19, 1938).

Women engaged in manual or service work are also shown in the advertisements, but with significations of 'boyishness' and a crisp cheerfulness which may well have been oppressive and/or offensive to the real workers of the day, as in the following example: 'Did you Maclean your teeth today?' The question is partly addressed to the reader and partly to the unsmiling face of the uniformed female elevator operator presented behind the bars of her lift, and above the caption.

'On the level, I did!' Her now smiling face in second image with peaked hat at jaunty angle peers out from behind the elevator gate which she has pulled to one side. The uniform visible—hat & braided collar—seem to signify masculinity, a military association, whilst the connotation of femininity is present in the use of cosmetics—glossy lips, nail varnish, soft wavy hair (*Woman*, April 9, 1938).

Products previously sold primarily to men, for example cigarettes, often retained the masculine frame of reference, even in women's magazines. The selling point of masculine recommendation or association with the product seems to be used as a tactic for exploring (and exploiting) the new female market. An advertisement in *Woman* showed two figures smoking cigarettes—a young woman sitting at grandad's feet—with the caption: 'Goldflake is the man's cigarette that women like' (*Woman*, February 26, 1938).

This stamp of male approval seems to be an important element in the review articles of the period. Nigel Graham, a regular feature writer for *Woman*, looks out, smooth haired and smiling, in a large photograph heading his article 'Should women give up their jobs?'. His recommendation is that women who like their jobs should continue working after marriage and 'not degenerate into a paid housekeeper' (*Woman*, April 30, 1938). Graham's column invariably focuses on a theme of how women should present themselves to men, with the added authority that the advice is offered by one who has the 'inside story' on such matters—a man!

'The good wife is the person who never forgets she was once Miss X. With all that Somebody's interests and enthusiasms and individuality which won her husband's love.'

Nigel Graham continues this line of advice in an article which poses the question 'Why is it that the best of women often become the worst of wives?' His concluding remarks reveal far reaching assumptions about the class position and educational experience of his readership:

'All the same, I do believe—and I think it's only common sense—that a man would rather be served with scrambled eggs by a woman who's done or read something interesting during her day and can talk about it, than with roast pheasant by a woman who's done nothing but roast it' (*Woman*, April 23, 1938).

Fiction in the magazines explores a wider range of variations on the theme of women in paid employment, although this is ultimately posed as the alternative, and nearly always least preferable, to marriage and motherhood. The narrative structure of the stories allows for considerable non-traditional, non-stereotyped behaviour in the characters during the

Fig. 2.   *Woman*, 9 April 1938.

central progression of the plot, with women often shown as non-passive, taking the initiative, breaking the rules, even the law, though perhaps only to 'get her man'. The contrast between independence and domesticity is often paralleled by other oppositions—wealth/poverty; city/country; leisure/work; extravagance, conspicuous spending/austerity; night life, sophistication/'simple' values.

A certain degree of social, political comment is occasionally present against, for example, the boss who pays low wages (*Peg's Paper*, June 1, 1938) or the difficulty of finding a job (*Lucky Star*, January 1, 1938). By the conclusion of most of the stories and serials, the iconic happy couple has reasserted itself, framed by the setting sun. An interesting analogy can be drawn here with certain Hollywood films made in the late 1930s and 1940s in which themes of independence (both economic and sexual), work and class position are explored, often foregrounding women as the central characters. As in the magazine fiction, these themes are generally concluded, and the 'problem' invariably resolved, by marriage which is often shown as bringing wealth and social status with it.

What explanation can be found for the image of the 'active' and often working woman in the magazines of the 1930s? One possibility may be that with the expansion of light industry at that time there were attempts to create a whole new market for domestic goods and the new household services of gas and electricity (Branson and Heinneman, 1971). Further indications of this can be seen in the advertisements for gas and electrical appliances, as well as in some of the documentary films of the period. John Grierson, for example co-produced 'Children at School' in 1937 for the British Commercial Gas Association, a film arguing for improvements in education and, in particular, in the material conditions of school buildings and facilities.

Obviously, this unexplored market at the end of the 1930s could only be found initially in the small but growing middle class. Women, as a group, however, were being addressed by the media both as potential consumers and as potential additions to the white collar labour force. The expansion of prestigious company offices and secretarial services at this time required a certain number of trained female staff, with of course suitable appearance, behaviour and aspirations. Staff entering the retail trade and especially the big stores were subject to similar demands by their employers. Mr. E., an ex-employee of a large London store, speaking of the staff selection process in the 1930s, told me:

'When you came to the store the men had to look a bit smart. The girls had to look young ladies. You see if you looked like a four ale girl, a bit tussled and that sort of thing, well, you wouldn't get the job . . . (the shop assistants) were nearly all working girls who had to earn their living, who had to get a job. . . . They were girls from good working-class and middle-class families. They looked and they were young ladies.'

Another employee of the same store, now retired, Miss A. told me:

'I knew what it was when I first went out to business to walk the West End looking for a job and there weren't the jobs. . . . You worked hard, you worked well in those days because if you didn't you'd be unemployed. If you were not a good worker you'd be out.'

Trade Unions were apparently disapproved of by the managing director. His view was well known and clearly presented a threat to job security for many employees. Resonances of such employers' attitudes seem to filter through in parts of the magazines. Trade Unions, for example are almost never referred to, and unemployment, except for occasional references in the fiction, remains invisible. The number of women in Trade Unions at this time was small and there are few reports of militancy or collective action in support of employees' demands in this sector of white collar work—actions may have been taken and gone unrecorded, or been 'hushed up'.

There is a concern in the magazines with manners and social custom which may indicate the role they played (and still play) as a guide to the behaviour expected by employers as well as a guide to prospective employees on how to present themselves. A model is constructed in the magazines of the kind of acceptable, largely middle-class codes of dress, speech, and behaviour which would enable a woman to get and with a bit of luck keep a job. Letters pages for example, have repeated requests for advice on the finer details of manners and the socially acceptable 'Do you shake hands or just nod when you say how do you do ?' The 'lazy' secretary is castigated in supposedly lighthearted articles on proper office conduct. This preoccupation in the magazines may indicate the workings of class and perhaps the notion of the passage from one class to another. The magazines, it seems, would certainly like to encourage the illusion of that transition.

It would be incorrect to suggest a simple relationship between economic change and content/presentation of the magazines. But in trying to make sense of that difficult terrain which covers the ground of traditionally separate areas of economic, political and ideological questions, one can at least attempt interpretations intended to draw these areas together historically.

The work of Klingender (1935) and deriving from this Braverman (1974) may be useful in this respect. A study made in 1935 of clerical workers indicated that an ideology of individualism, elitism and self improvement dominated many in this expanding area of white collar work, now drawing in larger numbers from the working class. According to Klingender, a shortage of jobs generally and a lack of traditional Trade Union organization in white collar jobs led to an acceptance of low wages allied to employer-generated pressure on workers to 'leave the working-class stigma attached to Trade Union membership behind them'. Vera Douie's survey of this period describes 'the creation of special classes of low paid women's work . . . fostered by the introduction of machinery for such processes as addressing, duplicating and tabulating. . . .' (Douie, 1943).

To the woman reader working in shop or office for low wages, the magazine presented simple, individualistic solutions: 'take the initiative but be a good worker', 'take the initiative and marry the boss's son if possible, if not, then marry the boy next door and give up work'.

We can note the ideology of individualism inscribed into the magazines, including the 'adventures' of the leading female characters in the fiction. We cannot be sure of how the women of the 1930s would have 'read' this. It is possible that an oppositional reading[4] might have separated out the images of independence and dynamism from the 'happy endings'. The exemplar of the image of woman depicted as taking the initiative, showing independence, may also be read as a way of finding confidence and standing up to the boss, or office manager, demanding better wages and conditions and rebelling against his equally oppressive and exploitative son!

4. WAR TIME: 'EVEN THE MORE SKILLED JOBS ARE NOT BEYOND YOU' (THOUGH THE WAGES MAY BE!)

An important reason for examining media artefacts produced under wartime conditions is that the relationship between the media and the State which is normally invisible is suddenly revealed.

Grieves (1964) maintains that women's magazines were the 'Cinderellas of the British publishing industry' at the start of the war. It is interesting then to learn that it was the Government which first recognized the potential of the magazines for communicating with

---

[4] For an elaboration of the notion of codes of audience and oppositional readings, see Stuart Hall (1973) 'Encoding and decoding in the TV discourse'. This is particularly important to the development of a theory of the media which does not treat the audience as passive receivers, or 'dupes' of all media messages.

large numbers of women. Grieves was one of the editors called in by the Ministry of Information in 1941 and asked to use their publications for two clearly acknowledged propaganda purposes: (1) to gain the support of women for the war effort and (2) to distribute government information to women. The editors were also consulted on Government policy matters such as the conscription of women and the effects of the arrival of U.S. troops in Britain, although here, concern was mainly about the effect on 'absent lovers and husbands' and not on the women at home. Even though the amount of advertising space and the overall size of the magazines was cut, the journalists still managed to retain the element of competitiveness regarding female appearance which is an inherent part of all 'beauty columns' and deeply rooted in the ideology of femininity.

With the collectivist ethic of the war effort, the tone of confidential but perky advisor is intensified:

'Don't let the girl next to you on parade get away with all the glamour. You're wearing the same uniform and Ann Edwards shows you how easy it is to look just as smart' (*Woman*, January 2, 1943).

The Women's War Service Bureau was a regular column in *Woman* addressed to working women, and clearly intended to boost morale and to make women feel more involved in the war effort and to maximize their potential as skilled replacements for the male workers then in military service. Unique exhortations, never repeated in peacetime, are made here to the readers to participate in social and political decision-making:

'The last joined apprentice in many a factory is a woman, it may be you, and although you may be a novice where engineering is concerned, there are many other directions in which you can be bright (and practical) and so help the war effort. Your working conditions, the clothes you wear for your work, the canteen and nursing services—all these are now admitted to be just as important as the most highly technical machine, and if you have any ideas on these, pass them on to the proper authorities' (*Woman*, January 2, 1943).

In the same column women are encouraged to offer themselves for training in jobs which in peacetime they would be excluded from and in which the wages for women would be considerably less than those for men:

'Here is a suggestion for helping production. Thousands of women are doing wonderful work in what are usually called the repetition jobs in factories. The skill they have achieved has surprised even the most broad minded instructors, but the time has come when women must more and more, do difficult jobs. Formerly it was the men who had been upgraded. This year must see women upgraded too. . . . There are two ways of upgrading yourself. One is to be trained by your own factory for a particular job; the other is to go to a govt training centre for the upgrading courses. These include turners, skilled fitters, machine tool setters, grinders, millers, die sinkers, auto setters, marine engine fitters, millwrights, maintenance engineers, fitters, and many others. These names do not mean a great deal to me, but you're in the factory already, and they should mean something to you. . . .' (*Woman*, January 2, 1943).

Again the direct address is used, personalizing this appeal for a more skilled labour force, though at the same time the magazine distances itself from any continuous association with the workers' experience of industrial production by pleading ignorance of technical terms— another way of incorporating the reader into an acceptance of an essentially peripheral role for women in the sphere of skilled paid employment, without of course detracting from the war effort.

The utilization of women's magazines to present a positive image of work outside the home for women also had the effect of reducing the emphasis on domesticity and the family, both in the ads and feature articles.

The sparkling, smiling faces in the illustrations signified happiness and fulfilment at work, with women dressed in boiler suits and dungarees and holding spanners and pitch forks. The advertisers found no problem in restructuring their 1930s image of women—in some respects adapting the 'career woman' stereotype developed earlier:

'Bovril doffs the cap to the splendid women of Britain' ran the caption of a series of Bovril ads, each with a different drawing of a woman in uniform drinking the product. The advertising copy here provides an interesting backup to the feature article geared to boost women's confidence, morale etc. and to expand the labour force.

'In every sort of war time task that women can do—and in a great many that women were never expected to be able to do—the women of Britain are scoring triumph after triumph. The services, munitions, the land, transport, hospitals, canteens, all bear witness to their skill and their courage. Bovril applauds these achievements' (*Woman's Friend*, February 1, 1943).

The selling point of household commodities becomes time saved to be used for war work. For example, an ad for Rinso washing powder depicts a female figure in dungarees and turban headscarf turning away from the kitchen sink and testifying: 'Me boil clothes? Not likely. I've got to be at the factory by two!'.

The image of the eager woman factory worker as presented in the magazines stands in sharp contrast to women's attitudes to war work as described in the Mass Observation report 'War Factory' (1943). Women in many industries during wartime did jobs which in peacetime were the exclusive preserve of men—and at a fraction of men's wages. The women in 'War Factory' worked a 12 hour day and understandably were often less than enthusiastic about the monotony of their jobs. One of the workers (Peggy) had been

'shifted around by the Ministry of Labour to a number of different factories. . . . She has disliked the work in all of them equally, but natural high spirits enable her to treat the whole thing as a huge joke. . . . The work itself bores her intensely, and her slapdash manner with the machine results in frequent breaking of drills. . . . In the same carefree spirit, she always wears nice dresses and stockings to work . . . "I'm not going to come in slops for anybody. I've always worn nice things to work and *they* aren't going to stop me".'

Little of this spirit of rebellion against bureaucratic control ever leaks out in the magazines. There are, however, moments when the editorials take up an explicit championing role between gallant woman war worker and monolithic but benevolent government machine: 'Give her this help' runs the headline in an appeal to organise homehelpers attached to hospitals to aid the housewife who may have to enter hospital as a patient (*Woman*, February 6, 1943). Whilst this has a populist ring to it, much in the tradition of popular national newspapers at the time, the campaigning on behalf of the readership could never extend, for example, to the question of wage levels. Even at the level of feature articles or letters pages nothing is published regarding protest actions over wages by women or about the lack of adequate nursery provision during the course of the war. There is no reference, for example, to the

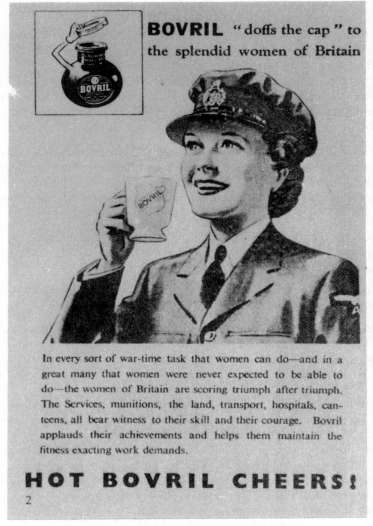

Fig. 3.   *Woman's Friend*, 1 February 1943.

strike of 16,000 workers at Rolls Royce in Glasgow in 1943 to get men's rates for the job applied more widely (see Calder, 1971). Similarly, the magazines make no mention of the 'demonstrations of mothers with prams' reported by Ferguson and Fitzgerald (1954) and resolutions from factories and housewives groups asserting the demand in 1941 for more nurseries.

Cynthia White (1970) maintains that the editors had more power over the magazines during the war period than at almost any other time—that in particular they were far less tied to the commercial/advertising pressures of later years. The ideology of the war effort and the explicit intervention of the State in media production were determinants on the shape of the magazines comparable to those of commercial/advertising pressures.

5. POST-WAR: THE DOUBLE JOB ROUTINE INSTITUTIONALIZED—'THE PROBLEM REFUSED'

Whilst in the fiction and feature articles of the 1930s and war period, conspicuous wealth, exotic lifestyles were often implicitly the subject of critical comment in the magazines, by the end of the 1940s the magazines were inserting the reader by proxy into that lifestyle of wealth and 'glamour'. Publicity catching parties were held by the magazines for the rich and famous to which a few readers were invited. The entire event would then be fed back in glorious technicolour photos as a voyeuristic feast to the absent readers for whose 'benefit' the party was ostensibly given. The intimate address ingratiatingly explains all:

'We have been to a party, and we wish you could all have been there. . . . If only we could let our readers into this we said. The River Room at the Savoy Hotel is pretty spacious but couldn't hold a million of you' (therefore six readers were invited). . . . 'There were celebrities galore and we made sure that our surprise guests met them' (*Woman's Own*, April 11, 1947).

Even the visual presentation reinforces a code of friendliness and informality, with a middle-page spread—in colour—of snapshot type photos showing the six readers chatting with 'celebrities', and a key giving their identities.

'We turn our heads to note Frances Day's oversize shoulder bag and feathered hat as she talks vivaciously to Beverley Nichols.'

The focus on elite groups, so characteristic of this type of feature, seems to become more predominant by the 1950s, and includes royalty on a regular basis. Features on weddings, childcare, fashion, cosmetics and 'homemaking' also became more prominent in the magazines and were largely geared towards restructuring the family unit and the woman's place within it.

The 'feminine mystique' was again foregrounded. It had always been there in the very structure of the magazines but was now given greater emphasis. Contradictory demands on women by the State in the post-war period manifest themselves in the magazines rather less on a total 'back to the home' emphasis and rather more on the equally exploitative and oppressive double job/dual role emphasis. The decline in population begun prior to the war was continuing and by 1947 was causing widespread alarm among the authorities with the publication in 1949 of the Royal Commission Report on Population, which recommended more material rewards from the State for motherhood and parenthood generally. Nevertheless, a female labour force was still urgently needed in certain industries, though in the women's press any paid work referred to tended to be white collar. (Women's bulletin from Trade Unions at this time, for example from the Amalgamated Engineering Union (AEU), are interesting both for their similarities as well as their differences from the commercially produced 'women's press'.)

The advertisements were not as work-oriented by the 1950s as they had been in wartime, but still show work situations, although generally in 'glamourized', traditionally feminine occupations—dress designer, air hostess, etc.

Feature articles deal more often than I expected with the difficulties of being a working wife. But at this historical moment when the economic and social formation required women to be both workers and mothers, and, most importantly consumers, the solution proposed is to buy more labour-saving goods—balancing

'extra money arned eagainst the amount of time to be spent in the home—there is a clear case for acquiring all that is necessary in the way of efficient tools' (Blair, *Woman*, June 24, 1950).

A 'reasonable' solution it might be said, if you can afford it! But not a solution which in any way deals with the problem of doing two jobs.

The editorial 'voice' captures the image of 'career woman' with a serious job to do in the photograph of her hands resting on her editorial papers at her editorial desk over the heading 'From my desk'. The address of cosy intimacy and informality is stronger than ever and this first issue of *Woman* in the new post-war larger size takes as the text of the day—'the family'.

'It's been rather like a family who after years of living in cramped quarters, suddenly find themselves in a house with room to turn round in. After the family have got over the shock of surprise and pleasure, they look at the fine empty rooms and decide how they will furnish them. That's what we've been doing—furnishing the new *Woman* with the help of writers artists and photographers. . . . I don't suppose you can have imagined the pleasure we've all had in re-making *Woman*, to give you back the extra value for your money robbed by paper rationing' (*Woman*, March 4, 1950).

The notion of team work is an important part of the mythology of the magazines spanning the decades: 'We've enjoyed putting this number together—we hope you'll enjoy reading it.' says the editorial of *Woman's Own* in September 1937.

The image of the magazine is as the work of a group of friends—mainly women—bringing together their individual skills and pooling these in a co-operative venture as informal and friendly as if the paste-up had been done on someone's scrub-top kitchen table. This image has maintained the seamless garment of the ideology of women's magazines—with no production processes, ownership battles and takeovers, sackings of personnel, advertising pressures, self-censorship by journalists, political attitudes, government advice, etc. . . only the voice of 'one of those friends we specially value, the ones who are always the same and always different'.

REFERENCES

Barthes, Roland. 1977. *Image, Music, Text*. Fontana, London.
Branson, Noreen and Heinneman, Margot. 1971. *Britain in the 1930s*. Weidenfeld & Nicholson, London.
Braverman, Harry. 1974. *Labor and Monopoly Capital*. Monthly Review Press, New York.
Calder, Angus. 1971. *The People's War*. Panther, London.
Douie, Vera. 1943. *The Lesser Half*. Women's Publicity Planning Association, London.
Drawbell, James. 1968. *Time on my Hands*. London.
Ferguson, Marjorie. 1978. Imagery & ideology. In *Hearth & Home: Images of Women in Mass Media*. Oxford University Press, New York.
Ferguson, Sheila and Fitzgerald, Hilde. 1954. *Studies in the Social Services*. U.K. Civil Series, London.
Fowler, Bridget. March 1979. True to me always. *British Journal of Sociology* XXX (1).
Grieves, Mary. 1964. *Millions Made my Story*. Victor Gollancz, London.
Hall, Stuart. 1973. Encoding and decoding in the TV discourse. Stencilled occasional paper No. 7. Centre for Contemporary Cultural Studies, University of Birmingham, U.K.
Hoggart, Richard. 1958. *The Uses of Literacy*. Pelican, London.
Johnston, Claire. 1975. *Dorothy Arzner*, British Film Institute, London.
Klingender, F. D. 1935. *The Condition of Clerical Labour in Britain*. London.
Mass Observation. 1943. *War Factory*. Victor Gollancz, London.
McCabe, Colin. Summer 1974 Realism. *Screen*, **15** (2).
Royal Commission Report on Population, 1949.
White, Cynthia. 1970. *Women's Magazines 1693–1968*. Michael Joseph, London.
Williams, Raymond. 1962. *Communications*. Penguin, London.

Winship, Janice. 1978. A woman's world: woman, an ideology of femininity. In: *Women Take Issue*.
    Hutchinson, London.
Wright Mills, C. 1956. *The Power Elite*. Oxford University Press, New York.
Zaretsky, E. 1976. *Capitalism, the Family and Personal Life*. Pluto Press, London.

Women's Studies Int. Quart., 1980, Vol. 3, pp. 79–93
© Pergamon Press Ltd.   Printed in Great Britain

0148–0685/80/0301–0079/$02.00/0

OVERWORKING THE WORKING WOMAN: THE DOUBLE DAY IN A MASS MAGAZINE*

Nona Glazer

Portland State University, POB 751 Portland, OR 97207, U.S.A.

(*Accepted June* 1979)

Synopsis—Portrayals of how employed women combine paid work and unpaid domestic labor in *Working Woman* magazine, a mass magazine, show women engaged in activities that support existing social relations between women and men, and between workers and employers, Individual solutions within the home are promoted. Personal life is adjusted to paid work. Women are portrayed as pursuing male-type patterns of success in the workplace: (1) while continuing traditional female work in the home; or (2) forgoing marriage and/or motherhood or minimizing personal attachments. Social solutions through co-operative actions or by reliance on the state are abjured for personal solutions that offer no or little challenge to existing social relations in either the public or private realm.

INTRODUCTION

I became interested in how the ideology presented in mass magazines might fit with the continued subordination of women while examining how various capitalist and socialist societies were or were not trying to solve the problems women face in combining paid work with unpaid domestic labor. This is the problem of the 'double day' or dual career as it is called in Western countries, or the 'second shift' as it is called in socialist Europe. The double day has been seen as a problem for women with family responsibilities (Glazer-Malbin, 1976); as a source of emotional and physical stress (Jancar, 1978; Glazer *et al.*, 1979) and as supporting women's continued subordination in the workplace (Rosen *et al.*, 1975; Fogarty *et al.*, 1971; Rapoport and Rapoport, 1976; Ginzberg, 1976; Kahne, 1978) and in politics (Flora and Lynn, 1974).

Research on the portrayals of women in mass circulation magazines has been notably atheoretical which describes most of the analyses of the mass media. Researchers do elaborate quantitative analyses without trying to relate their findings to theories (Jancus, 1977). The highly questionable assumption seems to be that how often women are shown with characteristics usually connected to men's special prerogatives is a measure of how far sex inequalities have or have not diminished. In contrast, I will try to relate the media portrayals of women to a broader view of women's lives. I will ask how portrayals of women, regardless of their new 'male' characteristics, may reinforce old sources of oppression and even create new problems for women. I will also give some attention to race, ethnicity and class as well as gender.

* Appreciation is expressed to Helen Baehr and Muriel Cantor (American University, Washington, DC) for most helpful editorial comments. I would also like to thank the librarians at the Business and Professional Women's Foundation in Washington, DC for their help in getting missing issues of the magazine and allowing me to have access to the most complete set in the area. I would also like to thank Lynne Dobrofsky for comments and Miriam Behman for editorial assistance.

Post-war research on the portrayals of women in mass magazines shows a change from a stress on women's family work and the family as the place for wives and mothers to spend their days to portrayals of women that include paid work as a regular if secondary activity. After studying magazines aimed at the homemaker, Franzwa (1974) concluded that for the period between 1944 and 1970, most did not show women as employed outside the home. Even single women were shown at home awaiting marriage. Usually, married women were shown as full-time housewives, and wives' employment was shown as potentially disruptive of a good marriage (Franzwa, 1974; p. 108). From 1955 to 1970, Franzwa found no married women shown as employed in the stories sampled. To Friedan (1963), the post-war image of the American woman in magazine fiction was 'the happy housewife', content to live a life centered on meeting her family's needs. Hatch and Hatch (1958) looked at the portrayals of employed women in magazines aimed at women who were more likely to be working outside the home than to be homemakers. They thought the magazines in 1956/1957 were 'unduly optimistic' about the problems facing employed married women. 'Techniques' were promoted as solutions to problems with children and home. The difficulties between wife and husband and the strains that the employed women themselves might be experiencing were ignored (Hatch and Hatch, 1958; p. 153). Franzwa concluded that paid work was shown as only of secondary interest to women who themselves only worked outside the home in exceptional circumstances, e.g. when married to a lazy husband. The women's movement had no apparent effect on attitudes towards women's domestic work and self-identity (Newkirk, 1977) or towards women's employment (Morelock and Kurth, 1974).

DOMESTIC LABOR AND FEMALE SUBORDINATION

Women's relegation to the private realm of the family and the household and hence to domestic labor, and their exclusion from the public realm of production, is one important source of women's subordination (Engels, 1902; Boserup, 1970; Sanday, 1974; Brown, 1973; Friedl, 1975; Rosaldo, 1974; Zaretsky, 1976). Yet, in neither contemporary capitalist nor socialist societies has women's entering paid employment outside the home had the predicted effect of liberating women (Mitchell, 1966; Rowbotham, 1974; Scott, 1974; Kuhn and Wolpe, 1978). Women continue to occupy subordinate positions in the workplace, to have less power than men in political life and to be marginal in the creation of culture.

A source of women's continued subordination is responsibility for domestic work, and the resulting long day of work. Research shows that women with families continue to do domestic work after entering the workplace, and that men and children do not increase their share of domestic work very much when wives/mothers take paid employment (Girard, 1958; Haavio-Manilla, 1971; Michel, 1971; Walker and Gauger, 1973; Meissner et al., 1975; Szalai, 1972; Hedges and Barnett, 1972; Berk et al., 1977; Robinson, 1977). This is also the case for employed women with family responsibilities in socialist societies (Szalai, 1972; Denich, 1977; Sokolowska, 1977; Jancar, 1978; Randall, 1979; Schwartz, forthcoming). One result of the double day is that many women are encouraged or forced to take paid jobs that are rightly or wrongly thought to be compatible with being a wife and mother first and foremost.

In capitalist societies, domestic work has at least two contradictory images: it is invisible 'nonwork', noticed only when it does *not* get done; and it is glorified as challenging and creative, the special province of women's special talents. Though men and children may 'help out', neither are thought to have the responsibility for the work, but only more or less follow out the directions of the woman of the household. This ideology has been understood as compatible with capitalism and with men's reluctance to do 'dirty work'. First, the invisibility of housework and child care relieves capitalists from any formal recognition in the wage packet of the labor that women do: maintaining a supply of workers by child-bearing, raising children and caring for (male) workers (Secombe, 1974; Morton, 1972). Hence, wages are seen as payment for labor in the workplace but not for the work of women in the home. Women who head families can be paid low wages without any recognition that they must do both paid and unpaid work, and cannot depend on a 'wife' as most men can. (Men also have higher wages than women and can more easily use the market-place as a substitute for the services of a wife.) Finally, reductions in the 'family wage' either through explicit wages cuts, or by a failure to keep wage levels in tandem with inflation, can be silently absorbed in the family by the woman increasing her labor. Women, for example, take on jobs that were once done by workers as when clothing manufacturers skip finishing steps in order to lower labor costs. Second, we have an ideology that justifies a social necessity—Galbraith's notion of the *convenient social virtue* (1973). Housework and child care which must be done can be avoided by men who enjoy the benefits of this 'dirty work' without confronting their avoidance as a way of either oppressing women or suppressing aspects of themselves. Instead, women's work is seen as natural and men doing such work as not natural, and perhaps even in conflict with men doing their own 'serious' paid work.

Why women continue to be responsible for domestic work in socialist societies has not been sufficiently explored. 'Patriarchical ideology and models' have been seen as survivals from pre-socialist modes of production, but why the survival has persisted for such a long time (over 50 years in the Soviet Union and about 35 years in Eastern Europe), and how this fits with the material organization of socialism itself still needs an explanation.

HOW EMPLOYED WOMEN DO DOMESTIC LABOR

The double day is a recognizable burden for employed women with family responsibilities. To see if and how the mass media recognized the problem, and if and what solutions were proposed for and to employed women, I examined *Working Woman* (*WW*) magazine. Issues of *WW* were read for all references to housework and child care.[1] Only advertisements were not read. This magazine which began to publish in November 1976 was chosen since it is aimed specifically at employed women, and promised in its first issue to deal with a wide range of issues.[2] The editors wrote that the magazine 'was created

---

[1] Twenty-six of 28 published copies were read for all references to domestic work. (Two issues were incomplete and unavailable even from the publisher.) Even tangential references to domestic work, objects, etc. were noted. For example, a discussion of warranties on garbage disposals was included as a reference to housework. If anything, therefore, the references to domestic work may be 'over-' rather than 'under-' estimated. Few references to domestic work were made compared to discussions of occupations, self-care (clothes, cosmetics, travel) and the use of money. The race, occupation, age, income and marital status of the women was noted when available, and two regularly appearing columns on occupations were examined to get some idea of the audience for whom the magazine might be intended. No attempts were made to establish categories prior to the actual reading of the articles.

[2] *The Audience.* An editorial (August 1977) reports that the readers are affluent, that 50 per cent are between age 24 and 39 years, that 54 per cent are married and 21 per cent divorced. Compared to American women in the work force, the readers have a higher income, are younger and more likely to be divorced. Yet the advice given to readers on occupational selection would not lead the readers—these women of the younger generation—to especially well-paid, politically powerful jobs. The readers are advised to enter accountancy, cab driving, real estate sales, photography, bar tending, typewriter repair services, and small businesses. Typical female-typed occupations are also promoted: dietician, secretary, nurse, medical records technical and travel agent. The women in the feature articles are, in contrast, in high level jobs in business or in the female glamor jobs such as actress.

to help women work out both the major questions that concern attitudes and ambitions, obstacles and expectations, as well as the ordinary bread and butter problems and pleasures of daily life' (*WW*, November 1976). An apparent response to the increased numbers of employed American women whom the editors called 'the next big spenders', *WW* was (January 1979) the only mass circulation magazine whose major audience was 'women who work outside the home' (Gebbie Press, 1978; p. 69 ff).[3]

What is 'domestic labor'?

References to domestic labor that emerged in my examination were as follows:

(1) parenting, including child bearing, breast feeding, daily care, transportation, super-vision of homework and leisure. Some parenting activities overlap with other kinds of domestic labor, e.g. cooking and purchasing are done by the employed woman for herself as well as for family members;

(2) cooking, including shopping for food;

(3) consumption, including goods and services for the family and the employed woman herself; and

(4) and general house maintenance, including cleaning, household repairs, 'straightening up', decorating.

How to do domestic labor

WW portrays women solving the problems of combining paid work with unpaid domestic labor through personal solutions primarily rather than social solutions. Personal solutions are those women work out by and for themselves, or with those in their families, or by turning to the market-place. These require no basic reorganization of the family, the market-place or the work-place. Social solutions include using the state's services (e.g. federally funded latchkey programs, free school lunch programs) most typically provided in socialist and welfare societies. Other social solutions include local co-operative arrangements with neighbors, fellow workers, members of the same religious, ethnic, racial groups for child care, credit, burial, home buying, etc. Finally, there are so-called alternative social in-stitutions that have been an integral part of the new women's movement—health clinics, shelters for battered women, bookstores, women's centers, etc.

The overwhelming reliance in *WW* on personal rather than social solutions suggests that the double day is a woman's personal problem. She has chosen to work or has failed to organize her life well so that she must work. Now, she must figure out how to cope with this choice or the result of her failure by changing aspects of her own life: her standards, her use of money, her use of time, her relationships. In the discussion that follows, I include

---

[3] Other magazines are read by employed women, such as *MS*, *The New Woman*, *Redbook* and *Cosmopolitan*, each of which presents topics of special interest to them. *The Working Mother* (McCall Publishers) was issued in October 1978 and was eventually followed by a second issue in Spring, 1979. None of the other magazines have only or mainly employed women as their intended audience.

statements attributed to women[4] discussed in *WW* to illustrate portrayals of how domestic work is done (see Appendix).

Parenting. Employed women are shown as coping with being a mother adequately, or by forgoing being a mother. Few women are shown as having insurmountable problems combining paid work with motherhood. Women cope mainly by control over themselves or over the members of their immediate family, or by buying the labor of others as substitutes for their own. Hence, women are portrayed as relying on baby-sitters, children's nurses, housekeepers, etc.; on co-operative husbands; and by using their own time with maximum efficiency. To illustrate, a famous actress took only a week off after her child was born because 'other women looked after him' (March 1977; p. 34). A 'three-role woman [worker, wife, mother] swears by her housekeeper. She counts herself blessed if her boss is humane and praises her husband's "participation" ' (July 1977; p. 48). A banker with a trained child's nurse also depends on 'an understanding husband who enjoys sharing family care' (September 1977; p. 20). The employed woman is advised to make well-disciplined use of her own time and labor: to reorganize her use of time, to alter her standards (downward) by compromising, not expecting too much from husband, children, baby-sitters, and day-care centers (November 1977; pp. 77–80).

Women are portrayed as the family member who usually both manages and carries out child care though others may also do the actual work:

'. . . even in our supposedly emancipated times, working women probably [*sic*] have many more housekeeping and family responsibilities than working men' (May 1977; p. 27).

The employed woman is advised to make a time study of her morning household jobs so she can decide rationally what can be eliminated, given to others to do, or done at some other time. Some jobs should be done the night before so that the employed women will not be late for work. Those night jobs are added to cooking ahead, to supervising children's

---

[4] Women's actual employment *ca.* 1977/1978 and the jobs discussed in the magazine or held by the women portrayed in articles differ. The jobs represented in the magazine as the work that women do, or suggested as the work that women could do, were more varied, better paid and less likely to be female-typed and sex-segregated that what women actually do. Glamor jobs such as actress, writer, artist, television performer, editor; higher level management jobs in business and government; lower level management jobs such as office manager, franchise operator, accountant and owner of a small business were the jobs of the women shown in the magazine. Only an occasional blue-collar worker was shown, and rarely were women clerical workers, service workers, or retail sales workers shown . . . the typical female occupations in the American labor structure.

A regular column in *Working Women* was examined for the occupations of the featured women whose pictures were shown along with a few lines about each. Political women were mentioned most often, those elected or appointed to office as well as those born to the office; another sizeable proportion were in business, owners, chairpersons or members of boards of directors, top business executives. In contrast, the *New York Times* (March 11, 1979; p. 50) reports that only 278 women were directors, holding 398 positions on 342 boards. Many writers, poets, novelists, non-fiction writers were shown. Smaller numbers of entertainers–singers, actresses and TV performers–were pictured. While as many blue-collar workers were shown as politicians, the first were shown in group and the second in individual portraits. For those interested in actual frequencies, the distribution was as follows: $N = 154$ photographed women. Political women, $N = 25$; business women, $N = 22$; writers, $N = 22$; entertainers, $N = 15$; blue-collar workers, $N = 27$ with the groupings meaning there were $N = 16$ photographs. There were no service workers, clerical workers or salespersons except for Roslyn Carter's administrative secretary and a telephone operator who had run the switchboard at a New York hotel for 50 years.

homework and spending 'quality' time with them (which seems to mean giving the children one's undivided attention), relaxing with one's husband, studying to improve oneself for the job—all after having stayed late at the work-place to impress the boss with one's serious career dedication. Working mothers, however, are told that they may leave the office promptly at 5 p.m. provided that they let their bosses know that office work will be taken home, to be done that evening. Personal time has disappeared, and the portrait that emerges from this composite is of a most harried woman.

The portrayal of the employed woman is that of an extremely self-reliant person. A single employed mother advises efficiency. Women ought to pay attention to details and to organize time tightly. Hence, the writer recommends being assertive about appointment times, e.g. demanding that the physician's receptionist phones the mother if the office appointments are running 15 minutes behind schedule; the mother is to find a salesperson who know her taste in clothes and will accumulate garments so the mother can schedule a quick try-on stop; children's clothes should be bought by mail; groceries should be ordered by phone or by a list dropped off at the store; and the groceries are to be delivered and the cost charged (January 1978; p. 43ff). The advice is quite class-biased. The suggestions demand a position of social power so that people will be interested in being accommodative on an individual basis, e.g. phoning to say there is more than a 15-minute wait in the doctor's office. The suggestions also assume a sufficiently high income to allow full use of the market-place, e.g. expensive grocery stores that provide unusual services. Self-reliance is also stressed in advice about keeping family spending down by developing good judgement about when a visit to a physician is really needed (October 1978; p. 58ff). Margaret Thatcher, now Britain's Prime Minister, who expects husbands to be 'as sweet and giving' as wives says:

'I simply organize my time . . . As long as one plans the essentials and cuts out needless or wasteful activities, one can run a home and have an outside job, with time to spare.'

No mention is made of the income necessary for such organization, the cost of delegating activities to others, what 'wasteful' might mean, nor what one might do in an emergency. Personal time again disappears.

The only grim note on parenting is the portrayal of a divorced woman with three children who earns $125 per week as a secretary and gets $100 per week in child support payments. She must sell an old house in which the family now lives because she lacks the cash to continue living there. She depends on free school lunches and on all of the children's weekend meals being given to them by their father; on a clothes co-operative for children's wear; and on lots of hamburger and chicken to manage the large mortgage payments and $200 per month baby-sitting costs (February 1978; pp. 42–43). Only in this portrayal do federal services (i.e. free lunches) and co-operative services (i.e. clothes co-operative) figure as important.

Innovations in the work-place are interpreted as helping women to parent rather than as helping the sexes to share the activity, or relieving men of parenting. Hence, articles discuss flexitime as a way that mothers can have time for child care (and housework); day care allows mothers to continue paid work without interruption (August, 1977; p. 77). Women (not men) change jobs to be able to spend time with their children (November 1977; p. 84), and express thanks that owning their own business lets them parent by bringing their children to the work-place.

Life is not completely smooth for employed women. Women are portrayed as expressing complaints about child care. Mother's fatigue, weariness with family life and a lack of personal time are also mentioned (July 1977; p. 49). Dissatisfaction with having to stop paid work in order to care for a child, and intense exhaustion are noted as difficulties, though not insurmountable.

Factual reports, in contrast to the articles that focus on the lives of particular women, recognize that employed mothers face many problems. The lack of quality day care, the need for reasonable maternity leave, support for federal financing and/or regulation of day care are mentioned. The special problems of migrant farmworker's mothers who, lacking day care for their children, must take small ones along with them into the fields is noted, too (June 1978; p. 64).

Not all employed women are shown as willing to attempt to cope with the problems of parenting. Their solution is not to have children. For these women, personal life and work life are portrayed as having been weighed against each other. Potential problems of children (and marriage) disrupting a career and/or their lives with a partner is solved by forgoing parenting. A permanent relationship may also be forgone. Thus, though many married women are shown in the work-place, and the days are supposedly long past when women (schoolteachers, airline stewardesses, federal civil service workers) are forced by the law to decide between family life and paid employment, many women are still portrayed as seeing these as alternatives. A married 27-year-old account executive says that 'children don't figure in their plans though they intend some day to have them, but don't want to discuss it now' (June 1977; p. 69). A 31-year-old assistant treasurer and her husband reportedly think it is easy for two adults to share housework, and though they plan to have a family, think it will be difficult (September 1977; p. 20). A television executive only agreed to marry 5 years ago with the understanding that 'she should remain in New York and not have children' (October 1977; p. 27). A married engineer would never consider having children 'if it meant stopping work' (February 1978; p. 31). Marriage is also portrayed as possibly disruptive of a career by a newspaper editor in her mid-twenties who has not yet 'ruled out the possibility of marriage and a family' (December 1977; p. 72).

Throughout the portrayals of parenting, the problems are shown mainly as those of the employed women rather than of men and women alike. The solutions are personal rather than social. Except for a mention of day care as a partial responsibility of the state, or of some co-operative efforts by parents, women are shown solving the problems of child care by a reorganization of personal life or a use of personal money. Flexitime in the work-place is rarely portrayed as a solution. When it is, the increased productivity of the worker is emphasized over social responsibility for children.

Cooking. The frequency with which cooking is discussed suggests that it is a major life activity. Though special articles on children appear in the first eight issues of the magazine only, 42 articles appear on cooking; recipes, advice on snacks, party-giving recipes and recipes for other kinds of entertaining. The employed women's problems of the double day are recognized in the advice about the details of scheduling special events involving cooking; shopping lists are published to help the reader prepare easily to follow the recipes. However, husbands and children are only portrayed as being marginally involved in cooking. Thus, children are given one recipe. Otherwise, they are not included in food preparation. (I should add that children are not portrayed as helpers except in articles that do not focus on housework, e.g. children are shown as doing chores in an article on minimizing the pressure of Christmas giving (December 1977; p. 46).) Men are absent from the kitchen with only one column presenting recipes by the three men who use them.[5]

Shopping. Woman's traditional job in industrial capitalism as the consumer–shopper is emphasized (and is also one reason—if not the main one—for the publication of the magazine). Several articles and one editorial point out that women are important spenders— 'the next big spenders'—who control large numbers of consumer dollars. However, women are not shown as mainly consumers for households, the neoclassical economists' and advertisers' usual view of women consumers. Women, instead, are 'individual' consumers, buying goods and services for themselves: clothing, cosmetics, travel, and financial investments. The articles assume working women have high incomes and the time to spend those earnings on pleasurable purchases. Expensive clothes, travel abroad, investments in items that require high incomes are featured.[6] Inconsistently, women are also assumed to be naïve about money with the most basic advice being given, e.g. on how to open a checking account, and find a bank that has convenient hours.

Satisfactory consumption is achieved by personal rather than social means. Women are urged to control costs and inflation by self-control. Hence, women are advised to limit their use of medical services to the essential, but they are not advised to lobby for price-freezes in medical costs, for a socialized medical system or more consumer control over the medical system (October 1977; p. 58). Some social means of controlling consumer goods are suggested such as labelling of goods, interest rate regulations and unit pricing (October 1978; p. 49; November 1978; p. 32). However, women are specifically warned to stay away from broader economic issues, from considering inflation and unemployment, and urged instead to 'stick to women's issues'— abortion, rape, day care, sex discrimination in credit and in the work-place (May 1977). Finally, articles on beauty, home decoration, etc. are really thinly-disguised advertising copy: products are promoted, and advice is printed about cost and availability. The seller's interest rather than the buyer's is foremost.

General household maintenance. Housework itself is never treated seriously as a topic by itself. Instead, the two articles that seem to be about housework are actually both humorous pieces. The references to housework scattered through the accounts of women's daily lives are similar to those on parenting. Hired help, a co-operative husband, the reorganization of personal time, the lowering of standards, full use of the market—these are the solutions that the employed woman is advised to use or portrayed as using to solve the social problems generated by the double day.

---

[5] The three men that demonstrated their cooking abilities in the Family Affair column were as follows: a husband whose family had a housekeeper, and who cooked on special occasions; a husband who cooked on weekdays, and whose wife cooked on the weekends, when she did quantity cooking 'for the freezer' so that the man's responsibilities during the week are unclear; and a husband who was a 'passionate chef'—the men are hardly models for sharing housework with their wives on the basis of equity, nor as a symbolic message to women that cooking is something that any man can or should do.

[6] The clothing shown is expensive: a $90 blouse, a $110 caftan, a $280 coat. The illustrations are incompatible with the earnings of the women shown. A woman working on trains is shown wearing a $95 skirt with an $80 sweater while a college student wears a $170 tunic outfit, and an airline stewardess wears a $100 skirt and sweater, and a $228 suit. Even outfits from discount houses are expensive: $179 and $165 for outfits, and one low-priced $42 suit.

DISCUSSION

I would characterize the portrayals of women's double day as supporting the following:

(1) the accommodation of personal life to the work-place;

(2) the unequal extension of work between women and men;

(3) the trivializing of housework (though not of child care);

(4) the interpretation of public issues as being personal troubles;

(5) the avoidance of class, race and ethnic issues;

(6) the encouragement of personal and non-political solutions rather than collective (co-operative and/or state-supported) solutions that depend on political actions.

Personal life and the demands of the work-place

Compared to earlier studies of women in mass magazines, women in *WW* are shown as concerned with jobs and careers, not just family life. Personal life is in fact adjusted so that women can be in the workplace. However, the organization of the workplace has not changed to allow women with family responsibilities support for fulfilling those at all easily. That direction of accommodation seems to be basically accepted in the portrayals even though women may not be completely satisfied. Women are shown as investing a good deal of time and energy in managing the combination of paid and unpaid work. They give up leisure, forgo marriage, limit dating, and do not have children in order to have satisfying paid work. What Hochschild (1971) has called 'the clockwork of the male career' seems to be accepted without question about how this may distort personal life. There is only a playful recognition that in most male careers there is a wife who carries out the important work of house and child care as well as giving the husband emotional support.

The unequal extension of work

Women in the work-place, contributing to family income or as the sole support in a one-parent household are taken for granted. There is no discussion of whether or not women should be at home rather than doing paid work. But the portrayals do not take men's sharing domestic work with women for granted. Instead men's doing domestic work is treated as problematic, difficult because men are so heavily involved in their careers, or it is treated as unusual, a special contribution of men who are enlightened. Hence, a man writes that men should support employed women by doing housework and child care 'not to help out but to do what needs to be done'. But he warns that men may experience pain 'from sharing the menial [sic] tasks of housework and parenthood' (December 1976; pp. 38–39). Men's work-place responsibilities are portrayed as having priority over family responsibilities and over women's need to have their men do half of the family's domestic work. A writer explains that while her husband 'tries to do his part . . . he can't help out [sic] as most husbands can't no matter what is said about "joint responsibility" ' (May 1978; p. 52). Women say that their husbands can sabotage careers, that 'there is no way on earth any ambitious women could perform well if she were married to someone threatened by her success' (October 1977; p. 50). Women are portrayed as having mixed feelings. A career woman and her husband share all household duties, yet she 'says with a sly grin: "My husband thinks he is liberal. I think he is just fair" ' (February 1978; p. 31). Ambiguity also emerges in what sharing means. A professional says she expects her husband to do 'equal amounts of housework' and then goes on to equate some of her husband's occupational activities with her doing domestic labor. Finally, she says: 'Anything that gets done in this house, I do' (April 1977; pp. 37–38).

The factual information presented in *WW*, in contrast to the portrayals of particular women, holds out little expectation that husbands can actually be depended upon for help or sharing. Hence, a study is cited as having found 'women use flexitime to take care of their children and housework while men use it for recreation and self-improvement activities, (November 1977; p. 84). Women are reported not only to waste less time in the work-place than men do, but 'when they go home do most of the housework' (November 1977; p. 13). Another study is quoted to show that employment for women does not mean a shift in who does domestic work nor an increase in women's power in the marriage (August 1977; p. 74), and fatigue (June 1978; p. 44) and a lack of time (November 1978; p. 35) are noted as serious problems. Finally, a well-known economist questions whether men really share housework and child care with women (November 1978; p. 35).

Trivializing housework

Housework as distinct from child care is only treated seriously when it is *cooking*. Clean-ing, laundry, home repairs, shopping for family rather than personal needs, the care of family pets, etc. are never considered as topics on their own. Also, many topics are com-pletely missing: the care for the elderly, and keeping kin and friendship ties going are well-documented women's activities, but are never mentioned as responsibilities of the employed woman. Housework is treated humorously or as easily done with some sensible thought and/or use of money.

Public issues as personal troubles

Personal life is seen as relatively disconnected from the public realm. Women are shown as solving problems largely through their own special talents or resources. No hint of the critiques that radical or socialist feminists have made of housework and child care arrange-ments and that have become incorporated into the mainstream of the women's movement appear in *WW*. Only in the sense that there is some attention to how men might share domestic work with women is there any recognition of the many issues raised by the movement.

Gender

The portrait of the labor force that emerges is one in which women face discrimination. However, that can be overcome by serious individual dedication to the job, getting appro-priate training, and being assertive, etc. Women are shown as modeling themselves on male professionals though that may not be made explicit. Women are urged to get new job skills and to enter the corporate world as secretaries from which position one can allegedly work up to executive positions. The meaning of sex stratification is underplayed by lauding as successful those women who are actually in middle-level positions, e.g. vice-presidents of minor departments in small firms. Women in top or middle positions in the female intensive industries of banking, insurance and advertising are portrayed as if they have broken major barriers and have extensive power. Small businesses are portrayed as a route to success. Thus, the small restaurant, the franchise, and the one-person business are featured without any discussion of the high risks involved and the high failure rate of small businesses. The absence of more than a few women from top positions in corporate America, the federal government, the military, etc. is ignored while the relatively small successes of women receive much attention.

Class, race and ethnicity

Class, race and ethnicity are absent from the portrayals of employed women while much of the advice given would be of little use to working-class women. The relevance of capitalism, corporate policies and the multi-nationals to sexist as well as racist practices in the work-place is completely ignored. Instead, the vast majority of women shown in illustrations in *WW* are white (as are the women in the advertisements). The fact that the women who do the 'dirty work' of housework and child care for pay so that other women can enter the work-place for well paying jobs are, of course, mainly minority women. How the double day effects these women who literally do 2 days of domestic labor on an average working day, for low pay, without fringe benefits, with no chance for advancements, etc. is absent from the magazine articles. Black and other minority women are invisible women doing invisible work.

Personal and collective action

What is absent from the references to housework and child care is as important as what is included. What is included are individually worked out solutions to what are implied to be personal domestic problems. What is missing or rarely mentioned are solutions that involve co-operative actions, e.g. neighborhood or community-based services. The state is seen as only a minor source of possible relief, e.g. in a legally shortened working week (16–28 hours). At the same time, the somewhat more collective solutions are legitimated by linking them to increased productivity in the work-place rather than to improving the quality of family or personal life. Thus, flexitime is promoted as a way of giving women more time with their families, but it is acceptable because it will decrease absenteeism and the time lost in coffee breaks (March 1977; pp. 74–77; August 1977; p. 77; November 1977; p. 84). There is no sense in which women workers are seen as having the right to a personal life that may infringe on corporate profits.

Political quietism is encouraged, too. Women are *not* shown as politically active in order to improve their lives. Political action—through women's movement organizations, traditional women's groups such as civic betterment associations, political parties, neighborhood associations, unions or professional associations—is not part of the lives of the women portrayed in the magazine. Even relatively mild political action, such as writing to members of the U.S. Congress about legislation on day care, is posed cautiously.

CONCLUSIONS

The portrayals of employed women in *WW* are supportive of the continued subordination of women. If responsibility for domestic work is interpreted correctly as a major mechanism limiting the liberation of women in the work-place, politics, the creation of culture, in interpersonal relations between the sexes, etc., then the women who appear in *WW* have acquiesced in their continued second-place position in American society.

The portrayals of how employed women do domestic work are by no means completely consistent. There is a contrast between the lives of the women featured in the story-like articles and the more factual columns about research, court decisions, etc. The former show women who are usually well-paid and who cope readily with the double day. They have done so without more than minor, if any, changes in the organization of American society. The latter recognize the problems that women face in doing domestic work as well as the discrimination women face in the job market. The editorials, too, are inconsistent or at least fail to make connections between different aspects of women's lives. Thus, one editorial comments on how 20 million American women support themselves and/or husbands and children even though they are in low pay jobs with short career ladders (February 1977). Yet another editorial states that inflation and unemployment (which hit women harder than others because of the segmented labor force that accounts for low pay jobs) is of no special concern to women who are urged to stick to 'women's issues' (May 1977).

The portrait that emerges is of women who cope with the double day easily, who do so without any basic reorganization of the work-place, without any far-reaching recognition by society of domestic labor, and without any challenges to the sex and age division of labor in the family. The implications for the readers is that if other women can do it, then they should be able to do so, too!

Employed women are portrayed as in the following models:

(1) *The Sponge Woman*. I prefer this term to 'superwoman' because it captures that essential component, that women absorb new responsibilities, again and again, without dropping old ones that were part of a quite different daily life. Some women have long combined paid and unpaid work in this way—poor minority women, immigrant women, women suddenly widowed, deserted or divorced. Now, that model is being presented to all women. Sponge Women, as portrayed in *WW*, take on paid work while continuing the same old home jobs, managing to combine doing domestic labor with working long hours outside the home, being efficient, self-demanding, by really accepting a speed-up.

(2) *The Deputy Woman*. The Deputy Woman retains the responsibility for the organization of domestic work, but others such as hired helpers, commercial organizations, or a husband carry out the actual work. The woman herself may do some work, but mainly it is delegated.

(3) *The Forgoer/Careerist Woman*. This woman is a sociological male, portrayed as following an exaggerated version of the male whose dedication to paid work means a personal life that is minimized. The Forgoer fits marriage and children around the demands of her career; and she is portrayed as having accepted this way of life without any sense of loss.

The portrayals of employed women in *WW* are an enforcement of privatized domestic work, in which the individual woman is responsible for housework and child care. There is no recognition that the problems facing women are socially generated, that women are being asked to do two jobs simultaneously. There is no questioning about the justice of the demand. There is no recognition that low family income and child support allowances pressure women to take paid jobs; that the organization of the work-place fails to consider that women workers have family responsibilities; that the organization of services, shops, recreational facilities, schools, etc. assume that most women are full-time housewives, not paid workers. Rather than any suggestion that there is a social source to women's problems, the double day is shown as a personal problem. Women, in turn, are shown as solving that problem by personal means: by an intensification of work, by delegating work to others in the family, by hiring helpers or otherwise turning to the market. Women even forgo social relations in which the responsibility for housework and child care might be disruptive of careers and/or personal relations. The re-emerged women's movement attempted to show how the personal is political. The portrayals of women in *WW* have reversed the tie: the political has become personal.

APPENDIX

All of $N = 396$ articles were read. This included $N = 25$ editorials, $N = 156$ departments and $N = 42$ cooking columns. The magazine has no fiction, but the treatment of topics is usually personal rather than general. Hence, single motherhood is examined via portrayals of the lives of several single mothers rather than by a general discussion of the status. The magazine presents general information in a few columns that are a pot pourri of factual items, e.g. 1–3 sentences summarize a Supreme Court ruling. The amount of total magazine articles devoted to housework and child care is shown in the tables below.

Table 1. References to housework and child care in regularly published columns

Title	No. times printed $N = 156$	Format*	Housework	Child care	Other†
On Top	24	N			
Working Mother	8	Q & A, N	2	all 8	
Looking Good	15	N			
Moneywise	22	N			
Your Mind, Body	21	N			
Power Play	13	N	2	2	3
Legal Briefs	21	Q & A, N ($N = 88$ Q & A)	1	13	4
Traveling Easy	12	N		1	
Working Your Way Up	20	Q & A ($N = 73$)	2	3	

* Format: N means narrative; Q & A means question and answer. N in parentheses refers to the number of occurrences.

† Other: references to pregnancy benefits, maternity leave, legality of a lease with concealed pregnancy, etc.

Table 2. Frequency of articles focusing on housework and child care
(Feature articles and columns)

Articles ($N = 396$)	Housework	Child care
Job, success, etc. $N = 354$	2	10
Cooking $N = 42$	42	—

Both articles on housework were humorous rather than serious. The only columns considering specific housework activities were the 42 on some aspect of cooking of which two involved persons other than the woman of the house.

REFERENCES

Bem, Sandra L. and Bem, Daryl J. 1973. Does sex-biased job advertising 'aid and abet' sex discrimination? *J. Appl. Social Psychology* 3 (1), 6–18.

Berheide, Catherine W., Berk, Sarah F. and Berk, Richard A. 1976. Household work in the suburbs: the job and its participants. *Pacific Sociol. Rev.* 19 (4), 491–518.

Blau, Francine D. 1979. Women in the labor force: an overview. In: Freeman, Jo ed. *Women: a Feminist Perspective*, pp. 265–289. Mayfield Publishing, Palo Alto, Calif.

Boserup, Ester. 1970. *Women's Role in Economic Development*. George Allen and Unwin, London.

Brown, Judith K. 1973. Leisure, busywork and housekeeping. *Anthropos* 68 (5), 881–888.

Denich, Bette. 1977. Women, work, and power in modern Yugoslavia. In: Schelegel, Alice ed. *Sexual Stratification*, pp. 215–255. Columbia University Press, New York.

Engels, Frederick. 1902. *The Origins of the Family, Private Property and the State*. International Publishers, New York.

Ewen, Stuart. 1976. *Captains of Consciousness*. McGraw-Hill, New York.

Flora, Cornelia B. and Lynn, Naomi B. 1974. Women and political socialization: considerations of the impact of motherhood. In: Jacquette, Jane ed. *Women in Politics*, pp. 37–53. John Wiley, New York.
1971. The passive female: her comparative image by class and culture in women's magazine fiction. *J. Marriage Family* **33**, 435–444.
Fogarty, Michael P., Rapoport, Rhona and Rapoport, Robert. 1971. *Sex, Career and Family*. Sage, Beverly Hills, Calif.
Franzwa, Helen H. 1974. Working women in fact and fiction. *J. Commun.* **24** (2), 104–109.
Friedan, Betty. 1963. *The Feminine Mystique*. Norton, New York.
Friedl, Ernestine. 1975. *Women and Men: An Anthropologists View*. Holt, Rinehart & Winston, New York.
Galbraith, John Kenneth. 1973. *Economics and the Public Purpose*. Houghton Mifflin, Boston.
Gebbie Press. 1978. *All-In-One Directory*, p. 69. Gebbie Press, New Paltz, New York.
Ginzberg, Eli. 1966. *Life Styles of Educated Women*. Columbia University Press, New York.
Girard, M. Alain. 1958. Time budget of married women in urban centres. *Employment of Women*, pp. 185–214. OECD, Paris.
Glazer-Malbin, Nona. 1976. Housework. *Signs* **1** (4), 905–922.
Glazer, Nona, Majka, Linda, Acker, Joan and Bose, Christine. 1979. The homemaker, the family and employment. In: Foote Cahn, Ann ed. *Women in the V.D. Labor Force*, pp. 115–169. Praeger, New York.
Haavio-Mannila, E. 1971. Convergence between east and west: tradition and modernity in sex roles in Sweden, Finland and the Soviet Union. *Acta Sociologica* **14**, 114–125.
Hatch, Mary G. and Hatch, David L. 1958. Problems of married working women as presented by three popular working women's magazines. *Social Forces* **37**, 148–153.
Hedges, J. N. and Barnett, J. K. 1972. Working women and the division of household tasks. *Mon. Labor Rev.* **95**, 9–13.
Hochschild, Arlie. 1971. Inside the clockwork of the male career. In: Howe, Florence ed. *Women and the Power to Change*. Carnegie Foundation, New York.
Jancar, Barbara Wolfe. 1978. *Women Under Communism*. Johns Hopkins, Baltimore.
Jancus, Noreene. 1977. Research on sex-roles in the mass media: toward a critical approach. *Insurgent Sociologist* **VII** (3), 19–32.
Kahne, Hilda. 1978. Economic research on women and families. *Signs* **3** (3), 652–665.
Kuhn, Annette and Wolpe, Ann Marie. *Feminism and Materialism*. Routledge & Kegan Paul, London.
Manpower Report. 1975. The changing economic role of women. In: Glazer, Nona and Waehrer, Helen Y. eds. *Woman in a Man-Made World*, pp. 85–98 (2nd edn, 1977). Rand McNally, Chicago.
Meissner, Martin, Humphrey, Elizabeth W., Meis, Scott M. and Scheu, William. 1975. No exit for wives: sexual division of labour and the cumulation of household demands. *Can. Rev. Sociology Anthropology* **12** (4), Part I, 424–439.
Michel, André. 1971. *Family Issues of Employed Women in Europe and America*. E. J. Brill, Leiden.
Mitchell, Juliet. 1966. Women: the longest revolution. *New Left Rev.* **40**, 11–37.
Morelock, Judy and Kurth, Suzanne B. 1974. Giving women what they want? the representation of trends in the role of women in women's magazines, 1956–70. Paper presented at the annual meeting of the Society for the Study of Social Problems, Montreal.
Morton, Peggy. 1972. Women's work is never done. *Women Unite*, pp. 46–48. Women's Educational Press, Toronto.
Newkirk, Carole Ruth. 1977. Female roles in non-fiction of three women's magazines. *Journalism Q.* **54** (4), 779–782.
Parish, Margaret H. 1976. Women at work: housewives and paid workers as mothers in contemporary realistic fiction for children. Dissertation abstracts. June. 77-7730-A.
Randall, Margaret. 1979. Personal interview. Havana, Cuba (January 1979) (Notes on Cuba. Nona Glazer.)
Rapoport, Rhona and Rapoport, Robert. 1976. *Dual-Career Families Reexamined*. Harper & Row, New York.
Robinson, John P. 1977. *How Americans Use Time*. Praeger, New York.
Rosaldo, Michele and Lamphere, Louise eds. *Women, Culture and Society*, pp. 207–222. Stanford University Press, Stanford.
Rosen, B., Jerdee, R. H. and Prestwich, T. L. 1975. Dual career marriage adjustment: potential effects of discriminatory managerial attitudes. *J. Marriage Family* **37** (3), 565–572.
Rowbotham, Sheila. 1974. *Woman's Consciousness, Man's World*. Penguin, New York.
Sacks, Karen. 1974. Engels revisited. In: Rosaldo, Michelle Z. and Lamphere, Louise eds. *Women, Culture and Society*, pp. 207–222. Stanford University Press, Stanford.
Sanday, Peggy. 1974. Female status in the public domain. In: Rosaldo, Michelle Z. and Lamphere, Louise eds. *Women, Culture and Society*, pp. 189–206. Stanford University Press, Stanford.
Schwartz, Janet. Forthcoming. Women under socialism: role definitions of Soviet women. *Social Forces*.
Scott, Hilda. 1974. *Does Socialism Liberate Women?* Beacon Press, Boston.

Secombe, Wally. 1974. The housewife and her labour under capitalism. *New Left Rev.* **83,** 3–24.

Sokolowska, Magdalena. 1977. Poland: women's experiences under socialism. In: Giele, Janet Z., Smock, Audrey C. eds. *Women-Roles and Status in Eight Countries*, pp. 348–381.

Szalai, Alexander. 1972. *The Use of Time.* Mouton, The Hague.

Textbook Study Group. 1972. Sex role stereotyping in Ontario primary readers. Regional Municipality of York, York, Ontario.

U.S. Civil Rights Commission. 1977. *Window Dressing on the Set.* U.S. Government Printing Office, Washington, DC, U.S.A.

Walker, Kathryn and Gauger, William H. 1973. The dollar value of household work. Cornell University Bulletin 60. Cornell University, Ithaca, NY.

Weitzman, Lenore J., Eifler, Deborah, Hokado, Elizabeth and Ross, Catherine. 1971. *Sex Role Socialization in Picture Books for Pre-School Children.* Mimeo. L. J. Weitzman, Davis, Calif.

Zaretsky, Eli. 1976. *Capitalism, the Family and Personal Life.* Harper & Row, New York.

Women's Studies Int. Quart., 1980, Vol. 3, pp. 95–104
© Pergamon Press Ltd. Printed in Great Britain

WOMEN IN LATIN AMERICAN FOTONOVELAS: FROM CINDERELLA TO MATA HARI*

CORNELIA BUTLER FLORA

Ford Foundation and Kansas State University, U.S.A.

(*Received and accepted May* 1979)

Synopsis—The *Fotonovela* is a series of still photographs with balloon captions, telling, usually in 30 pages, a complete romance. Its evolution as a separate genre of women's literature is related to the changing definition of women's world for working-class Latin Americans. The shift in the locus of production and the way it is structured nationally and internationally relate to potential profits and magazine content. Audiences have been growing to include men, which on the one hand unites men's and women's worlds, but on the other sharpens some negative female images, especially those related to sex and violence. Emerging from the Cinderella theme of the 1960s, two distinct types of fotonovelas are identified in the late 1970s: the *novela suave*, with middle-class pretentions stressing salvation through consumption, and the *novela roja*, with working-class characters, explicit sex and violence, and a social disintegration focus. The implications of these for women's passivity in various spheres is discussed.

Almost since the invention of the printing press, women's fiction has proved a lucrative venture. Middle-class women—women from the class that was literate and had the leisure and money to read—were avid audiences for the 'romantic scribblers'. From *Pamela* on, women formed a unique market for literature that was devalued as 'sentimental' and worthy of contempt, when considered at all. Yet women's fiction, both in print and in the electronic media, gives important clues as to the content, myths, and reality which construct the world of women, as contrasted to the world of men (Bernard, 1978). Women's fiction provides both a reflection of women's world, as defined by social class and cultural context, and a means of shaping it.

The women's world present in English language women's fiction has been relatively well-documented (Brown, 1940; Papashvily, 1956; Fiedler, 1960; Russ, 1973; Smith, 1974; Mitchell, 1978; Kelley, 1979 are all examples of literary critiques of fiction aimed at middle-class North American and British women). In the Hispanic world, the parallel to the sentimentalists and the gothic novels came on the scene at a later date, in the *novelas rosas* of such Spanish authors as Corín Tellado, which came out weekly and were distributed in both Spain and Spanish-speaking Latin America in cheap paperback editions. These have been analyzed as breeding false consciousness, through ahistorical plots ignoring economic and political reality (Erhart, 1973; Colomina, 1976; Paz ,1977).

The novel format, focusing on the printed word alone, limited the audiences of both the *novelas rosas* and their English language counterparts. Another media form emerged, which utilized visual as well as verbal images, creating a unique type of feminine literature, the *fotonovela*. The fotonovela is a series of still photographs with balloon captions telling, usually in 30 pages, a complete romance. It appears as a magazine or comic with a specific series title (such as Corín Tellado, Fotoromances, Pecado Mortal) and comes out usually

---

* A version of this article was presented at the Eighth Meeting of the Latin American Studies Association in Pittsburgh, Pennsylvania (April 5, 1979).

weekly or bi-weekly. In Spain, its immediate precursor was the *tebeo feminino*, romantic comic books that took hold in fascist Spain. According to Ramirez (1975), their success was due to their ability to deal with the major problems facing women as individuals in a society that was developing with profound internal contradictions which demanded certain compensations. The tebeos provided an escape. Romance as the ultimate reward for passive female behavior seemed the one sure thing in a world with uncontrollable, constant changes.

The fotonovela began after the Second World War in Italy, and later in France, as a by-product of the film industry (Haber, 1974). At first, the fotonovelas simply used stills from films, but soon evolved into its own media form, using the plots from novels written by Corín Tellado and the *tebeos femininos* which had preceded the war. A new way of creating the female world for working-class women appeared, which can be equated to the 'True Confessions' magazines in the United States (Flora, 1971). Even with low levels of literacy, the mass media were readily available to take their place along with religion and the family in defining what was ideally feminine—as well as ideally masculine.

At first most of the fotonovelas sold in Latin America were produced in Europe. Later subsidiaries of European companies were established in Latin America which printed the European product. Still later, Latin American-based companies began producing as well as printing the fotonovela.

In this article, the images of women presented in fotonovelas and their importance in reflecting the status of women in Latin America, particularly Colombia, will be analyzed. The structure of fotonovela production will be linked to the content and the different images of women presented.

CINDERELLA

Fotonovelas which circulated in Colombia in the 1960s and early 1970s were typified by *Corín Tellado*,[1] formerly shot in Spain and printed in Miami. They dealt with the sentimental problems of the high bourgeoisie (Mattelart, 1970). In them, Cinderella finds her prince. The heroine, poor, but somehow in middle-class quarters, with an upper middle-class wardrobe and beautician, maintained her purity and her pride in the face of pressures from males, both good (rich) and evil (not rich). Problems were solved through the passive acceptance of the heroine. Her virtue alone was sufficient to unmask the millionaire who had pretended to be poor to test whether she loved him or his money. Of course she loved him for himself.

Women in these stories were overwhelmingly passive, as demonstrated by their degree of dependence, lack of efficacy and initiative (Flora, 1973). Good women, those identified as supremely passive, had a latent sexuality, awakened by the hero and saved for marriage. Marriage appeared as a constant orgy of physical fulfilment with the steady arrival of

---

[1] Corín Tellado is the name of a Spanish author of romantic novelas. Originally she published cheap paperback novels of 127 pages, which appeared weekly. These were later converted to the fotonovela format, with the magazine entitled *Corín Tellado*. A television series (soap opera) of that name was distributed for a time. Other women's publications, such as *Vanidades* (published in Miami, U.S.A.) and *Paula* (published in Santiago, Chile) also publish the novelas. Corín Tellado is undoubtedly the best known female writer of the Spanish language, and her name, used as the title for one of the earliest and best known fotonovelas, became representative of both a person and a style of popular literature.

beautified babies, who *never* appeared in the fotonovela itself. There was occasionally sex outside of marriage for the good women, which was usually the result of being tricked by drinking too much alcohol. This was always instigated by the villain. She *never* enjoyed this illicit liaison. The double standard was strong, because men's sexuality could usually not be repressed. Indeed, the strength and degree of devotion of the hero was measured by his ability to somehow keep himself from physically violating the heroine when she appeared ready to 'give herself to him'. He, not she, was able to think ahead and maintain her virginity, which was her most valued possession. The women were either middle-class, or, because of their purity and passivity, worthy of becoming middle-class through marriage. Sex was implicit, scenes were chaste (indeed, the French and Italian fotonovela exporters shot special less suggestive love scenes in the 1960s for the Latin American market), and violence never appeared.

But changes in the Latin American situation, both in terms of production and consumption led to the demise of Cinderella. The novela format gained popularity in both its radio and television form. To compete, the printed form used its major advantage—the option of being more explicitly sexual. In Colombia, a growing economy and increasing rate of inflation required the economic input of women. The birth rate dropped dramatically. *Corín Tellado* and the sexually passive female vanished from the sales racks. The locus of fotonovela production for the northern part of Latin America moved from Europe to Mexico.

THE GLASS SLIPPER BREAKS

Currently in Colombia there are two distinct types of fotonovelas. The two genres can be distinguished by the amount of sex and violence portrayed. The first genre is the *novela suave*,[2] which is based on the fotonovelas that first came from Europe. Sex is a part of the novela, but it is not as explicitly portrayed. Violence is not a major element. The second genre is the *novela roja*, a more recent arrival in Colombia, which originated from Mexico. Explicit sex and sexuality, as well as constant physical violence, particularly of men against women, are the hallmarks of the *novela roja*.

While the covers of the novelas suaves strive for a romantic and tender note, using head shots or in a few cases shots from the waist-up of male and female characters in close and touching proximity, the novelas rojas always have full body shots, with the women either in the scantiest of bikinis or underwear or with strategically torn clothing. In 50 per cent of the cases, explicit violence or the threat of violence is shown on the cover. *Los Adolescentes*, a Mexican-produced fotonovela, when it does not show explicit violence on the cover, presents on the back cover what is advertized as a 'sexi-poster,' which shows women in even greater stages of undress and more suggestive poses. On these covers, female sexuality is portrayed as an irresistable temptation to men, leading toward sin and away from reasoned interaction and solidarity between the sexes. The violence portrayed reinforces the individualistic mode of problem solution. Mata Hari's sexuality inevitably leads to tragedy.

---

[2] *Novelas suaves* and *novelas rojas* are terms I am defining to represent the new current types of Latin American fotonovelas. The only similar term used in Spanish literary criticism is *novelas rosas*. In my development of the subject, I want to build on that term.

PRODUCTION

Both genres currently produced come primarily from Mexico, but there is a small but vital movement toward nationalization of the product with Colombian-produced fotonovelas. Some are coming out of Venezuela as well. The printing industry in Colombia is well protected through prohibition of importation of printed materials. All the fotonovelas distributed in Colombia must come through a Colombian editorial house, be printed by a Colombian press, and distributed by a Colombian distributor. However, there is no law concerning the *source* of the material, and in certain cases, it is much cheaper to buy the negatives ready to be taken to the press than to prepare the materials in Colombia. In one case although they could have shot the novela in Colombia at less cost than they could purchase the negatives, the parent company in Mexico insisted they purchase the Mexican product.

Because the costs of production are the same no matter how many times the negatives are used, re-use rather than national production is encouraged. In a show of independence, not nationalistic feeling, one Colombian editor changed the Mexican-produced covers for cover photos purchased from Europe, showing Nordic type protagonists in spring-like outdoor settings, unrelated to the content of the magazine.

The novela suave is a logical offshoot of the Corín Tellado format. There are no more millionaires for Cinderella to marry, but the characters are clearly middle-class. The males are destined for comfortable office jobs. The heroine is still often of slightly lower social class origins, often working as secretary for the male, who is older and more cynical, but eventually captivated by the heroine's endearing simplicity, purity, and groveling devotion.

The editorial companies producing the novelas suave see themselves responding to the Mexican fotonovelas, which they do not feel meet the needs of Colombian reality. The newly-installed chief of production at Editora Cinco recently wrote to Mexico asking them to change their themes to be more positive. She sees the Mexican products as very damaging, both regarding the themes presented and the abuse of language, which tends to be full of idiomatic Mexican phrases that do not fit Colombian word usage. She stated she felt a moral obligation to raise the level of the reading material in Colombia. She did not feel her objection to the Mexican product was a Puritanical one, but based on a realization of the differences between Mexico and Colombia. Particularly offensive was the large degree of machismo she saw present in the Mexican fotonovelas. The men in charge of production of the other Colombian fotonovelas are much less concerned about machismo in the Mexican product. Their complaints, when they exist, are that the Mexican fotonovelas are in general crude and destructive of Colombian cultural identity.

Production of fotonovelas is almost entirely male-dominated. All of the directors and producers are male. As in English language women's fiction, there is a relatively high female input into the story line with nearly half (45 per cent) of the listed authors having identifiable female names. Interestingly, in the current sample (1978/1979), no author is given in 27 per cent of the fotonovelas.[3] None of the novelas rojas are credited to women. Interestingly,

---

[3] In the course of my cross-national studies, I have found several of the stories *not* credited by author in their Colombian incarnation did have authors in a previous Mexican existence. The titles and photographs were changed, but the captions and dialogue are identical. Obviously, there is little copyright protection for authors. The authors who were pirated without credit were, interestingly enough, women.

the most sexually explicit of the novelas suaves, *Extasis*, from Venezuela, are almost all written by women.

Unlike the novelas suaves, which use a variety of authors for different issues within the same title, the novelas rojas tend to have a single author for each title. Myths arise surrounding these authors, who every week come up with a story titillating enough to attract school boys on their way home from school, taxi drivers between customers, prostitutes during the day, and maids when the family is out. José de Cruz, who originated *Pecado Mortal*, the original novela roja, was said to have written it between two and five in the morning, standing at his typewriter in the dark. Apparently the hour and the obscurity inspired his lurid imagination.

AUDIENCE

The novelas suaves are aimed at a middle-and lower middle-class audience. The editorial houses have carried out rudimentary market surveys which show them as reaching a better-educated audience than originally anticipated. They see their magazines being bought by women, but read by women and men. Although profits come almost exclusively from the volume of sales, with numbers of copies printed in Colombia ranging from 19,000 to 70,000, (contrasted to around 300,000 for those printed in Mexico), several novelas suaves are beginning to attract a few advertisers as well. Advertising appears for entertainment (other novelas, magazines, television and radio channels, usually owned by the company or its subsidiary), but also beauty products (bras, hand cream, nail polish remover) and sanitary napkins. Consumption, the ads imply, leads to an increase in status. Sewing machines are advertised in a few numbers, emphasizing the possibility of working at home in one's 'spare time,' either by selling directly through a small *tienda*, or shop located in the home, or through an intermediary to a larger clothing manufacturing company. Such machines are often sold on credit, for substantial down payments and weekly or monthly payments. In many cases, machines are repossessed and sold any number of times, for the home sewing business is not as lucrative as indicated in such novelas as *Simplemente María*, and small enterprises prove to be very risky to the woman investing, although profitable to those selling the machines. The ads for self-improvement fit nicely with the themes of the novelas suaves that indicate the importance of self-improvement, through study or deliberate individual actions. They suggest ways of earning necessary income while at the same time retaining the woman's primary identification as housewife.

The editors of the novelas rojas see their audience as decidedly working-class or even lumpenproletariat. Their circulation is higher in Columbia than the novelas suaves—ranging from 50,000 to 75,000 copies per week, per title.

The content of the novelas rojas sells because it relates to what people see in real life. The mother who has been unfaithful, the betrayed country girl who turns to prostitution, the father who forces his sexual attentions on his daughter (always unknowingly in the novelas rosas) are something the readers themselves have experienced and to which they can relate. Men increasingly buy the novelas rojas primarily for its 'turn on' effect. But women keep buying it as well.

That convoluted sexual violence is indeed a part of the reality of even readers of the novelas suaves is indicated in the letters received in response to the advice-to-the-lovelorn column. The cases related are so horrifying and so complex that very few can be printed, much less be responded to in a rational and helpful manner. The novelas rojas do not solicit letters, but still seem to have a sense of reality of the life of the working classes.

The chief of production and his colleagues at Editorial Icavi in Bogota see the popularity of the novelas rojas as due to an increasing cynicism in Colombia. A less romantic generation, which has been raised with radio and television, sees the kind of romance that stresses chastity and tenderness as ridiculous. Movies containing nudity and explicit sexuality have changed expectations. Credibility of the press has fallen in Colombia, and newspaper sales have fallen. The drama of the fotonovela, touching as it does on the everyday conflicts of the lower middle and working classes, outsells the drama of national and international events.

USE OF SYMBOLS AND IMAGES OF WOMEN

A certain amount of moral hypocrisy is needed in the presentation of the novela roja, although it is also present to a growing extent in the novela suave. The bad people always lose, although they seem to have a great deal of fun on their way to perdition. Sacred symbols, such as God, family, motherhood, and, in the Mexican-produced fotonovelas, the virgin of Guadalupe, are brought in at crucial moments to help identify the good people. The symbols are both visual and verbal, with the pornographic and the sacred often presented in close juxtaposition.

Good–evil juxtaposition is most striking in cases such as 'A Debt to Pay' in the fotonovela *Pecado Mortal*. In a convoluted mixture of sex, robbery, sex, murder, and sex, Lydia is a prostitute-adventuress, the mistress of 'Flat Tire' who was foiled by the humble railroad watchman in a train robbery attempt. Mauro is married happily, if in poverty, for 10 years. He has a son dying of a brain tumor, who can only be cured by an expensive operation they cannot afford. Lydia becomes attached to Mauro after he finds her hiding in a railroad car, has sex with her, and befriends her. He tells her that if it weren't for his wife, he would certainly form something more permanent with a hot potato like her. Lydia arranges by trickery to get stolen money to Mauro, and have her lover arrested for the crime. The story ends with the statement that '. . . God, the Allpowerful, had moved her bitter heart'.

The juxtaposition of symbols serves both to justify the reading of the story, since it has after all a moral lesson, and to justify the lives of those who read it, who suffer the same realities of forced sex, physical violence, and dependence on faith to survive. The format of sinful actions, but retribution at the end, is not unique to the fotonovela. In countries like Brazil and Chile where military censorship keeps sex and violence out of the media, religious television and radio programs often play the same role. A new convert comes forward to tell his or her story, urged on by the evangelist. Sins are enumerated, and, at the urging of the evangelist, elaborated at great length and glowing detail, often for 15 or 20 minutes, beginning after the opening hymn and lasting until time for the closing commercial. In the last 30 seconds the converted sinner quickly remarks that Jesus saved him or her, and he or she hasn't engaged in any such awful behavior since salvation. The act of being titillated by the recounting of sins is justified by the final moving of the Hand of God.

In the fotonovela there is a long, often violent and exploitative story which serves not so much to develop the plot, which is usually set down in the first four of the thirty pages, as to keep the reader's interest and present the qualities of good and evil which allow for problem solution. The solution comes on the last two pages, generally through the convenient, although usually violent, death of one of the protagonists. (See Martinez Pardo, 1978, for analysis of these variables in television.) This is like the lotteries, which for the poor in Latin America represent the swift, uncontrolled solution to complex problems that cannot be simply solved. The solutions appear not as a natural consequence of the preceding events, nor as the voluntary action of the principles involved, but as an act of fate. Violence and death are much more likely to be the solutions in the novelas rojas, which are consciously aimed at the lower income market and more likely to include scenes of poverty and working-class living quarters as part of the story development. For these individuals, all efforts at self-improvement are likely to be impeded by the social structure, and thus fate is much more likely to be emphasized as paramount in determining people's lives.

The fotonovelas rojas give an *appearance* of contact with reality, through the mention of educational problems, problems with work, problems of romantic fulfilment, and, in the case of the 'true life' stories, with the sex and violence surrounding everyday life. But, this appearance deals only with the individual level, and thus serves to mystify the situation to give the impression of a solution. The simple solution presented, in the presence of so many details that may appear real, can tend to obscure an economic and political analysis of individual problems and to focus on escape and passive waiting, rather than organization and active attempts at change. The novelas suaves have 'real' problems as well, but, unlike the novelas rojas, they are emotional rather than economic in origin. Thus solutions are more easily worked out. There are not the economic complications as presented in the novelas rojas.

WOMEN AND PASSIVITY

Women in fotonovelas remain moderately active economically. In 1 1970 survey of foto-novelas (Flora, 1973) as in 1978/1979, 50 per cent were either employed or studying. In a 1979 survey, there were significant differences between the novelas rojas, where few worked, and the novelas suaves, where more women were employed. Yet it remains clear that the most important role for women, linked closely to their sentimental role in keeping the man from evil, is in their role in reproduction of the labor force. The women are never employed in jobs of consequence or high earnings, although those that are prostitutes occasionally are shown to receive temporary high remuneration for services rendered. In the novelas rojas, half of those women who were shown as employed were prostitutes, while the rest of those employed used or were used for sex as a direct result of their employment. In the novelas suaves, the women were secretaries or students.

When the woman is not economically active, she is reimbursed ideologically. She helps her husband, is loyal to him, despite mental, physical and economic mistreatment, ulti-mately receiving the prize beyond value—a man of her own. The male is mobile and untied to family needs, and thus suited to an advanced economy, while the woman is tenaciously loyal, providing emotional stability in a situation where other stability is systematically denied.

The novelas suaves are much more likely than the novelas rojas to show plots being happily resolved through individual action rather than through fate (no collective action of any kind occurs). The most common 'action' is when the woman (70 per cent of the cases) or the man (20 per cent of the cases) remains faithful and awaits the love who is dealing with a barrier. It is usually another emotional involvement, including (1) a sexual rival, obviously more promiscuous than the hero or heroine; (2) a prior emotional claim, either a mother (in the case of men) or a child (in the case of women) who does not allow them to get together, or (3) the pride of the man who fancies himself to be a playboy and thus must be tricked into realization of his love for the heroine. Only in this last category does the heroine act, instead of react, and it is her natural goodness, in combination with the involuted plot, that results in the hero giving up his life of one night stands and adoring women. In the other two categories action more usually resolves the plot than a random act of fate. However such action tends to be the dramatic revelation of wickedness in the sexual rival or mother. There are certain fateful interventions in the novelas suaves that make the barrier between lovers disappear—a mafioso shoots the cruel husband as he leaves jail on drug charges; a priest tells the heroine in confession that it is not a sin to marry her dead twin sister's widower; the woman's first love, crippled in a construction accident, dies in order to free the woman from caring for him—but the majority of novela suave plots have an internal logic and systematic resolution. But active women still imply destruction.

WOMEN AND SEXUALITY

Sex has come out of the marital chamber and hit the beaches, the woods and other romantic and not so romantic locations in both types of fotonovela. Even nice girls have sex and they do not necessarily wind up pregnant. Occasional affairs within marriage are tolerated, if they serve to (1) bring the married couple together, or (2) establish a loving relationship prior to the demise of the cruel husband (divorce is discussed, but never occurs: death always precedes legal action).

A sexually active female, provided she acts out of love, is no longer automatically wicked and to be punished in the novelas suaves. A common theme is the fallen woman raised—a woman who made a mistake for love (but the man turns out to be vile and abandons her, with or without child), confesses all to the gentle and loving man who marries her anyway. Honesty, rather than purity, has become the new sexual criterion.

In the novelas suaves, women authors are more likely than men to deal explicitly with sex. Sex appears explicitly in 50 per cent of the stories credited to men, and in 66 per cent of the stories credited to women. Women authors are more likely to deal with extra-marital, as opposed to pre-marital sex.

Female sexuality in the novelas suaves is part of the plot. Almost all the novelas rojas have on their opening page a couple in a passionate embrace, his hand under her miniskirt. The angle used for the photography is a low one, emphasizing the legs of the female protagonist. The last shot usually shows the dead body of the female protagonist, again shot from the legs up, where she has fallen after being brutally murdered by the hero in mistaken jealous anger.

Female sexuality in the novelas rojas is omnipresent, and is no longer a means to label a woman as good or evil. Evil women use sex, and good women are either (1) true to one man, in or out of marriage, or (2) used by men for sex. Female sexuality, however, in a majority of the novelas rojas, is seen as the major source of evil, inspiring violence and breaking down primary ties to the point of fratricide and patricide. The linkage of sex with violence—woman, by *being*, inspires the worst in men—makes inevitable the incest and rape that follows. Even in the novelas suaves, the incest theme is evident, with fathers invariably, although unknowingly, desiring their illegitimate daughters. As Memmi (1968) pointed out, it is the thing that most intimately identifies a woman—her sexuality—that makes her most vulnerable to oppression. This vulnerability is given in the novelas rojas.

Women are powerless, and suffer violation and death with the same passivity they were awarded the prince in the Cinderella tales.

Insanity is a common plot device in the novelas rojas that allows for some sort of coping with the violence, usually sexual, that women suffer. Like death, it becomes the only manner of dealing with an impossible situation. Both the dead woman and the mad woman achieve a beatification that poverty usually denies. They are both the ultimate conclusion to marianismo, machismo's other face (Stevens, 1973).

MATA HARI

In previous work on fotonovelas, Jan Flora and I identified three types of fotonovelas: (1) total escape; (2) disintegration–integration; and (3) consumption as salvation (Flora and Flora, 1978). The total escape type with its Cinderella heroine has practically disappeared from the Colombian scene, although a few still exist in the novelas suaves. The consumption as salvation type also appears in a more muted form in the novelas suaves. In Colombian fotonovelas the consumption item stressed as key to all others is education, with much stress laid on the necessity of the hero continuing his studies, despite his impulse to marry and get a job right away to support his wife and future children. The message is 'wait, study, and have an even better life'. With the waiting, sex before marriage is acceptable, although it must be confined to the intended or attributed to a brief losing of one's self-control, usually as a result of grief or alcohol. In the novelas suaves that portray married couples, the consumption as salvation form is more explicit. Usually the marriage is suffering because the husband is stingy both with his money and his attentions. Through the intervention of an attentive rival, usually a creation of the husband to see if his wife is really faithful and loves him, he learns by her warm and passionate response to the generous man of fiction that he has erred in his ways by not spending more, with the monetary and emotional expenditure being equated.

Most common is the disintegration–integration type, although, particularly among the novelas rojas, disintegration prevails. There Mata Hari and female destructiveness prevail. While fotonovelas have always denied the existence of community, union, or political groupings, now even the family is shown as a source of danger from which the individual must be separated. The incest theme separates fathers from daughters, daughters die bearing the father's child, and sons and fathers kill each other in battles over the son's wife. Love for the same woman (usually wicked and manipulative) causes brother to kill brother. And even the mother–child bond is broken as the mother-in-law increasingly becomes the wicked manipulator who keeps lovers and husbands and wives apart. It is more the novelas suaves which deal with the wicked mother theme, while the novelas rojas focus on the wicked results of ill-directed male passions. Sexuality isolates the woman from her family, who, upon discovering her immoral behavior, throw her out with curses and blows.

CONCLUSION

Fotonovelas have become more 'realistic' as the genre of women's fiction has shifted from Cinderella finding the prince to Mata Hari losing everything.

However the message of female passivity has remained the same. Once produced for a single audience, the fotonovela presented a single dream of escape. Now with a readership that cuts across social classes, two distinct subgenres are emerging: one aimed at a middle-class audience (novelas suaves), and one aimed at a working-class audience (novelas rojas).

Both subgenres now recognize female sexuality and explicit sexual content has led to an increasing number of male readers. Sex and violence become equated in fiction as they are in life.

Changing patterns in production and changing cultural settings may lead to more options for middle-class women, sexually if not economically, and these are represented by the novelas suaves. But for working-class women, the solutions to the real binds of both economy and machismo are limited and dismal: madness or death.

REFERENCES

Bernard, Jessie. 1978. Models for the relationship between the world of women and the world of men. In: Kriesberg, Louis (ed.), *Research in Social Movements, Conflicts and Change*. JAI Press, New York.

Brown, Herbert Ross. 1940. *The Sentimental Novel in America*. Duke University Press, Durham, N. C.

Colomina, Marta. 1976. *La Celestina Mecanica*. Monte Avila Editores, Caracas.

Erhart, Virginia. 1973. Amor, Ideologia y Enmascaramiento en Corín Tellado. *Imperialismo y Medios Masivos de Communicacion*. Casa de las Americas 77, 93–101.

Fiedler, Leslie. 1960. *Love and Death in the American Novel*. Criterion Books, New York.

Flora, Cornelia Butler. August 1971. The passive female: her comparative image by class and culture in women's magazine fiction. *J. Marriage Family* 33, 435–444.

Flora, Cornelia Butler. 1973. The passive female and social change. In: Pescatello, Ann (ed.), *Female and Male in Latin America*, pp. 59–85. University of Pittsburgh Press, Pittsburgh.

Flora, Cornelia Butler and Flora, Jan. L. Winter 1978. The fotonovela as a tool for class and cultural domination. *Latin American Perspectives* 5, 134–150.

Guillermoprieto, Celma, 1977. El Caballo del Diablo Un estudio de Caso. Paper presented at Primer Simposio Mexicano, Centroamericano de Investigación sobre la Mujer, Mexico.

Haber, Angeluccia Bernardes. 1974. *Fotonovela e industria cultural: estudio de una forma de literatura sentimental fabricada para milhoes*. Vozes, Petropoles, Brazil.

Kelley, Mary. Spring 1979. The sentimentalists: promise and betrayal in the home. *Signs* 4, 434–446.

Martinez Pardo, Hernando. 1978. *Qué es la televisión?* Bogotá, D. E. Centro de Investigación y Educación Popular, Serie Controversia No. 67.

Mattelart, Michele. March 1970. El nivel místico de la prensa seudo-amorosa. *Cuadernos de la Realidad Nacional* 3, 221–283.

Memmi, Albert. 1968. *Dominated Man*. Orion Press, New York.

Mitchell, Sally. 1978. Sentiment and suffering: women's recreational reading in the 1860s. *Victorian Studies* 21 (1), 29–45.

Papashvily, Helen Waite. 1956. *All the Happy Endings: A Study of the Domestic Novel in America, the Women Who Wrote It, the Women Who Read It, in the Nineteenth Century*. Harper & Bros, New York.

Paz, Ida. 1977. *Medios masivos, ideología, y propaganda imperialista*. Cuadernos de la Revista Unión, La Habana.

Ramirez, José Antonio. 1975. *El Comic Femenino en España*. Editorial Cuadernos para el Diálogo, Madrid.

Russ, Joanna. April 1973. Somebody's trying to kill me, and I think it's my husband: The modern gothic novel. *J. Popular Culture* 6, 666–691.

Smith, Henry Nash. Spring 1974. The scribbling women and the cosmic success story. *Critical Inquiry* 1, 47–70.

Stevens, Evelyn P. 1973. *Marianismo:* the other face of *machismo* in Latin America. In: Pescatello, Ann (ed.), *Female and Male in Latin America: Essays*, pp. 89–102. University of Pittsburgh Press, Pittsburgh.

Women's Studies Int. Quart., 1980, Vol. 3, pp. 105–114
© Pergamon Press Ltd. Printed in Great Britain

0148–0685/80/0301–0105/$02.00/0

HE ADMITS . . . BUT SHE CONFESSES

Penni Stewart

York University, Downsview, Ontario, Canada

(*Accepted September* 1979)

Synopsis—Confession is an expressive act in an expressive language. It implies moral culpability and punishment usually involves re-education of the self. In contrast to confession, admission recognizes only technical error involving at most a loss of trust. No reference to self-culpability is necessary when one admits.

In this paper, three models of confession are presented and contrasted to a model of admission. The argument is made that confession is a female mode of response, reflecting women's position in the private world of home, while admission is more typical of males reflecting their position in the public world of work. This theme is illustrated through an examination of popular confessional literature such as *True Story* and *True Confession* magazines.

Confession as a mode of expression is as old as written history. Originally a religious act forming an essential element of the Judaeo-Christian tradition, it gradually became secularized and incorporated into the legal and literary cultures of the modern era. But whether religious or secular, the constituent elements of confession are the same: acknowledgement of guilt, judgement by others, punishment, and a return to respectability.

Confession may be contrasted to the modern trend of admission of error found in cases where contractual obligations are broken. In these cases, transgressions may be 'settled' without a statement of self-guilt (i.e. no fault insurance). While confession implies moral culpability, and punishment usually involves the re-education of the person, admission of the broken contract implies only a loss of trust and is usually punishable by a fine, without reference to the character of the defendant. Confession is an expressive act, in an expressive language. Admission, representing the profane or secular domain involves recognizing error, frequently *technical* error or use of inappropriate means. Both are mechanisms of social control complementing each other.

Whereas men tend to use admission responses to manipulate social relations, women tend to confess, although the two types of responses overlap. The language of confession is an emotional one, more familiar to women than to men, expressing women's location in the private world of home.* Confession implies shame, humility and submission, an emotional rather than cognitive orientation to the world. In contrast to this, admission reflects men's position in the public world of work. Admission recognizes a fear of loss of trust, of reputation in civil society and as such does not expose the self to the degree that contrition and expiation do. There is no moral submission to judgement when one admits as John Dean did to the Ervin Committee:

'I'm not here as a sinner seeking a confessional, . . . but I have asked to be here to tell the truth and I have always planned at any time before any forum to tell the truth (Dean, 1976; p. 321).

---

* As Robin Lakoff (1975) has pointed out, women's speech and language differ substantially from men's. Women tend to use weaker expressions, be excessively polite, use questions rather than statements. Lakoff argues that these differences are a result of women's position of powerlessness within the social structure.

Confession for men becomes a last resort, a recognition of failure of means rather than ends. As Dean points out, Richard Nixon never confessed:

'I went to sleep trying to figure it out. The cover-up had been a stupid error. Lying about it had been deadly for him. It was over now. He'd been caught in his lies, so why didn't he confess? Was he really far wiser and shrewder than most would give him credit for? Would history say he'd been unfairly forced from office? Was he planting seeds of doubt? or did he fear prosecution and jail?' (Dean, 1977; p. 361).

In the remainder of this paper I will be looking more closely at this distinction between admission and confession, particularly how confession is related to the female subculture as portrayed in popular literature and admission to the male subculture. Both response patterns will be contrasted with the personal growth pattern found in therapeutic and consciousness-raising confessions.

THREE MODELS OF CONFESSION

To confess is to reveal one's self, to remove the protective layers of self-justification and make one's self vulnerable. It includes risk as secrets are brought forth and anti-social acts made open. But with the risk comes the potential for emotional growth as defences are shed, and self-truths bared. This potential is the potential of maturation, of knowing oneself, a prospect not realized in admission, nor of course, through all confessions.

Using the notion of a potential for self-growth as a base we can distinguish three 'ideal types' of confession; the 'plea', the 'therapeutic confession' and the 'consciousness-raising' confession.

The plea is the classic stratified model of confession derived from the religious tradition of prayer in which the penitent humbly begs forgiveness from her confessor, and voluntarily submits to, or may even seek, the punishment expected or rendered. The purpose of the plea is to restore respectability, the usual place in the existing social order. As we shall see, there is little scope for self-growth with the plea. Rather, it expresses the infantile fear of loss of love. Redemption is only possible when others, the superordinates, are convinced of the sincerity of intention. As we shall see in our examination of popular confessional literature, the plea is the most common model of female confession, reflecting women's position of subordinacy, their dependence on affective manipulation, and their rootedness in primary group relationships.

The therapeutic confession finds its expression in the psychiatric model of patient–counsellor interaction. There is no judge; the therapist is expected to be broadly tolerant, if not value-free. The judge is internalized by the patient as conscience. However, to the extent that the therapeutic confession locates the nature of the problem in the individual, it, like the plea, is conservative. But whereas the plea expresses resignation to the world, the therapeutic confession is made in the hope of recreating the self.

While therapy attempts to resocialize, the consciousness-raising confession seeks a radical transformation of reality. Peers are substituted for the expert in the therapeutic relationship and for the authority in the plea. Through public confession to peers the individual develops a new definition of self, from one that is guilty to one that is unfairly oppressed (Bartky, 1977). The nature of social reality comes to be seen in a new light. Events and relations once accepted become for the confessee the tools of oppression. The individual who has gone through consciousness-raising gains a new self in and through a new concept of citizenship.*

While all confessions are self-revealing, of the three models, consciousness-raising calls for the greatest risk of rejection by others because it is always public. Everyone is the audience. While the plea may be the expression of private torment (an anonymously published diary, or use of a pseudonym) and the therapeutic confession a 'shared' secret, consciousness-raising must be public. Change in this model can only occur once you are 'out of the closet'.

We will return to a consideration of these three models of confession later, but first we will turn to a look at how confession has been used in popular literature.

THE GROWTH OF CONFESSIONAL LITERATURE

Just as the State took over confession from the church, literature took over confession from prayer and private religious ritual. And as the masses acquired literacy in the nineteenth century, the confessional theme became a staple of the new popular culture (Weibel, 1977).

In the twentieth century, the popularity of 'confessions' among consumers of both high-brow and low-brow literature continues unabated. Indeed, the recent popularity of biographical writings of all types suggests that the commodity value of confession may be on the rise. The popularity of the confessional theme also receives reinforcement through the television production of soap operas, which incorporate confession as a staple dramatic item although in a different format to that used by literature. As the author of a recent magazine article titled 'Hooked on soaps' says:

'Friday is the best day of the week for soap operas. Friday is full of da-*da* music and leading lines like, "It's time I tell you the truth about your father," da-*da*, or "Brad, there's something I must tell you," da-*da*' (Moore Campbell, 1978; p. 102).

In newspapers, syndicated advice columns are replete with anonymous, unsigned confessions of wrongdoing.

Although both the therapeutic and consiousness-raising models of confession are dealt with in the literature of confession, the plea, as we have already indicated, is by far the most common model. This is because the plea has a particular relevance to women's lives as they are described in the confessional literature, particularly in the 'professional' confessionals such as *True Story*, *Real Confessions*, *Modern Love Confessions* and *True Confessions* magazines which form the background for the following sections.

CONFESSION IS AN EVERYDAY EVENT—THEMES OF CONFESSIONAL LITERATURE

Just as the language of confession is one of emotion, the themes of confession found in popular literature such as *True Story* and *True Confession* magazines deal with the problems of emotional life. The overwhelming theme of the confessions is transgression, often transgression of emotional norms, as in confessions of culturally inappropriate rage, jealousy, or frustration. Occasionally, the confessions are of impulsive acts—abortion, theft or infidelity. In general the confessions are 'larger' than life, revealing a discrepancy between the norms of reality and the norms of women's lives as portrayed in the literature, where even the fantasy of transgression is a sufficient sin to prompt a confession.

---

* Kincaid (1977) notes that research shows that consciousness-raising groups have had three main effects: (1) women come to see themselves as more competent following the group; (2) they become more career/job-oriented; (3) there is an attempt to develop internal sources of self-identity.

The themes of the confessions appeal to their reader's concrete attachments. There is no aesthetic distance to these stories. But if there is a kind of crude illiteracy about them, it only adds to their credibility. None of the stories requires the reader to go beyond the borders of usual or possible experience. Aimed primarily at working-class or rural women the literature deals largely with problems arising out of relationships with family, neighbours and sometimes employers. Empathy with the confessee is easily evoked. For example, in 'I stole for my baby' a young, unemployed, single mother shoplifts on the advice of a friend in order to make some quick money. She tells the reader that she only listened to her friend because she was desperately lonely:

'It was easy to talk to Stella, and soon it was as if we had been friends for a long time. I realized how lonely for adult companionship I was. So I grabbed on to Stella Henning, and she didn't seem to mind a bit . . . I found myself telling her things about Vince and me . . . Both of us in our own ways, expressed our bitterness with the way life had treated us. We had always tried to do right but it didn't seem to help. Then Stella was suddenly telling me about how she picked up a few extra dollars—in fact quite a few dollars' (*True Story*, December 1977; p. 13).

In this passage, three themes common to the confessionals are captured. First, there is the notion that women are morally frail, doubly illustrated in this example where both temptress and victim are female. Second, there is the notion that life is an unrewarding, lonely struggle, one in which a trusted companion is rarely found. Finally, there is the belief that women are powerless, unable to cope with the malevolent forces of the world. As Nora says: 'We had always tried to do right but it didn't seem to help'. Moral frailty of women is a recurring theme of the confessionals, illustrated by the willingness of the confessees to take on denigrating self-images of irrevocable 'badness'. In 'Cry in the night' a young mother kills her avowedly insane husband in self-defence, following several years of constant abuse, but in her own eyes deserves ongoing punishment:

'But it did happen. And even though I am free in the eyes of the law, I will carry guilt on my soul for the rest of my life. I'm with my parents now, and I'm grateful for their goodness to me. Later on, I hope to find a job to support myself and the children. As for the future—I only pray that I can be a good mother to my little girls. If I can give them a happy life, wipe out the terrible memories that still shadow their eyes, I ask for nothing more. *As for Larry—and our dream of love—I've forfeited that forever. That is my secret punishment and no less than I deserve.* God grant me the strength to bear it' (*True Story*, Spring Romance Special, 1979; p. 101).

While human companionship is seen as likely to be untrustworthy and unrewarding, religion is presented as providing peace and fulfilment. A consistent backdrop to many of the confessions is that rejection of religious beliefs lead to punishment and that reinstatement in the social order is dependent on renewing ties with God. Otherworldliness is stressed as the only solution to a sordid reality. In keeping with this theme, most volumes offer some variant on a 'Miracle of faith' story.

These themes of frailty, moral struggle and passivity have behind them more fundamental messages about the lives of women. These deeper themes suggest: (a) that men have more rights than women; (b) that women are masochistic; (c) that women must resort to affective manipulation to gain legitimate ends; and (d) that female life is rooted in primary group relationships.

Men in the confession magazines are portrayed as having more freedom and immunity than women. They have the right to 'take what they can get', to impregnate and abandon without fear of punishment, to use women as objects for their pleasure. The machismo of men is a given, an accepted premise. The principle of *caveat emptor* is uppermost, and women who engage in pre-marital intercourse and become pregnant are seen as doubly guilty, first for having broken a still accepted moral code prohibiting intercourse without marriage, and secondly, for having the poor judgement to trust a 'bad' man, one who is already married or just 'congenitally' single. The responsibility always devolves on the woman. For example, when the young heroine of 'What the neighbors don't know' discovers that she is pregnant by a man who is already married, no thought of revenge enters her mind even though he had deliberately duped her.

'Our love affair didn't seem wrong, either—not with Larry making such plans for us to marry. And then I found out he already had a wife, that he'd just been stringing me along. I never saw him again' (*True Story*, Romance Special, 1979; p. 71).

Discrimination in judgement or the choice between a bad 'un or a good 'un is the central paradox for women in the confession magazines. Men are presented as both the cause for grief and the reward for confessing. In the example given above, not only does the heroine willingly shoulder her shame, but eventually gains a husband through confessing it.

' "I want to marry you more than anything in the world" I whispered brokenly. "But I can't." And then because I didn't know how else to do it I blurted out: "I'm going to have a baby. And its father—is another woman's husband. Now you can see the kind of person I really am." I closed my eyes, bracing myself for angry, accusing words. The next moment he was holding me close in his arms. "Poor little girl", he crooned softly. "I knew you had something on your mind all this time. Now that you've told me you'll feel better" ' (*True Story*, Romance Special, 1979; p. 71).

Further illustration of the double standard is found in the case of a woman who, when faced with her husband's demand to marry a virgin, is forced to lie in order to keep his love:

'I stirred uncomfortably in the bed, pushing back the old memory that tried to come at me. I could never tell Tom about it now. And I never wanted to think about it again. It was over, gone. Tom thought he had married an old fashioned girl—he loved to call me that in fact' (*True Story*, January 1978; p. 6).

Clearly the expectations in this relationship are not equal since there is no question in this wife's mind that she wanted to marry a virginal man. Both husband and wife seem to agree that it was her duty alone to remain pure.

Women in the confessional tradition are masochistic, consistently rejecting reality in the face of romantic love. Theirs is a consciousness of victimization without a realization of oppression. A woman's lot is hard but inevitable.

'It was good to let out all those aching things and give them air that day. Both of us, in our own ways, expressed our bitterness with the way life had treated us. We had always tried to do what was right, as we were taught by numerous teachers, priests, family members, but it didn't seem to help. We just went further down' (*True Story*, December 1977; p. 53).

Revenge is not permitted or even considered in the confessions, and statements of self-hatred abound. Thus a middle-aged mother of two children, without an occupation and threatened with divorce because her husband found a new younger lover, turns her anger against herself by attempting suicide, and accepts that she is neurotic for trying to keep her husband.

The resolution for women is found in cementing new dependency relationships. Thus confessions are often made to men, with the reward for confessing found in either the rebirth of a relationship or the development of a new bond. When Nora (heroine of 'I stole for my baby'), overwhelmed with guilt and fear, is driven to the brink of desperation, she turns to her friend Carlos to confess:

> ' "Oh Carlos, it's not you!" I wailed. "It's everything." And then out of nowhere out of fear, desperation, loneliness whatever, I was telling him about everything—about the shoplifting, about being caught, even about the humiliating experience with the store detective . . .' (*True Story*, December 1977; p. 58).

With Carlos by her side, Nora is able to resolve her shoplifting habit, and as a result of both the confession and self-improvement wins Carlos.

Independent action is not seen as suitable or even possible in many cases for women. Nor is action in concert with other women possible. Many of the sins portrayed are in fact against other women—sister, mother, best friends. While other females may be sympathetic good listeners, they have no resources to support the guilty female either economically or emotionally—they are in the same boat. Generally, emotional and physical worlds are privatized to protect the male's domain. Even on the job women are portrayed in confessional writing as isolated from meaningful contact with other adults. Whether on the factory floor or in the secretarial 'pool' the accepted norms of conversation are limited to social or maternal topics. Women's chief task is to socialize their young and thus the significance of adults or issues outside the family or domestic realm is minimal.

Security for women in these stories can only be achieved through manipulation of affection. Denied access to successful occupational role models, and without the financial, intellectual, or attitudinal resources for job training, these women become adept at manipulating men in order to ensure some standard of living. No effort is spared to keep their husband's interest, or to attract a 'good' man's fancy, and to avert the intrusion of a rival woman. Thus in 'A hypnotist taught me to enjoy married love' a woman confesses that out of fear of 'bruising' her husband's ego she was unable to relay to him her dissatisfaction with their sexual relations.

> 'I kept thinking Rick would realize that something was wrong—catch on to my act. But a man's idea of his ability to satisfy his woman's ego is a touchy thing. And I was really afraid of bruising Rick's ego . . . That's the way our marriage stood—even now, six months after the wedding' (*True Story*, November 1978; p. 20).

Much of women's lives in the confessionals is spent in self-examination or self-doubt, both physical and spiritual. The emphasis on purity and moral virtues so prominent in the confessions underlines this theme, for only with these qualities will women deserve male attention. Since they are perceived and perceive themselves as doing so little to earn their keep, they must expend great energy in maintaining their security through image making.

> ' "Come to the Complete Woman course with me "she cajoled. "It'll teach us how to organize things around the house, how to entice our husbands . . ."
> 'It sounded irrestible to me then. Efficiency and romance—what more could a harried housewife want? I agreed to go' (*True Story*, January 1978; p. 44).

For women in the confessional literature, life is rooted in primary group relationships; husbands, children, sisters, sisters-in-law, best friends, neighbors. This personalized, narrow world-view is learned through early socialization experiences. Girls are discouraged from learning the skills required to negotiate public life, to assume executive responsibility, to take on leadership roles. Instead, girls learn to be sensitive, to observe the feelings of others closely, to deal best with one-to-one interactions. The consequence of this lengthy affectional training is that the girl does not develop standards of self-esteem independent of others' expectations (Bardwick and Douvan, 1971). While teenage boys learn that self-esteem is based on achievement that can be measured tangibly, adolescent females learn to be 'feminine', to replace science with art and artfulness. The adolescent learns more-or-less successfully and more-or-less willingly to suspend her autonomy in favor of dependence (Bardwick and Douvan, 1971). The reward for learning this lesson successfully is to 'find' (or more accurately be found by) a husband willing to replace her father or some other authority figure.

As an adult, the woman exists in a no less personalized world, where being respectable or well thought of by others replaces other kinds of achievements except in the restricted area of domestic activity. Her adjustment to adult life is measured by her willingness to sacrifice self-fulfillment for the affection or well-being of family. Even for working women, their major concern rests with family and children, and family needs dictate the extent to which careers can be developed. Thus when Marcie, the central figure in 'I said no to my husband's job transfer' refuses to move with her husband because of her own career needs (the one case in the confessionals of a middle-class career—as a college professor) her friends and family are aghast. Marcie's story ends with a plea:

'Can you help this troubled wife? Do you believe she is right in insisting her career is as important as her husbands—or should she give up her own goals in order to be a full-time Wife? If you think you can offer her good advice, please write her . . .' (*True Story*, November 1978; p. 67).

WOMEN AS CONSUMERS OF CONFESSION

Women are the primary consumers of confessional literature just as they are the narrators. Readers can easily identify with the tellers who are 'ordinary' people with modest aspirations in life. There is a pseudo-kinship with the story teller whose background is vague—not too rich, not too poor, and whose language is informal and intimate. The reader is both voyeur and actor who recognizes in the narrator her own guilty conscience. The narrator acts out what the reader has felt. The very ordinariness of many of the acts confessed gives dramatic meaning to very undramatic events and at the same time emphasizes how close we all are to serious sin in our compromises with absolute morality. The reader of these magazines enters a fantasy world where all human experience is dichotomized as good and bad.

The confessions found in magazines like *True Story* and *True Confessions* provide an illusory relief to isolation. The reader and the narrator form a para-social bond, and both become part of a larger community. But the confessions do more. They are a response to the denial of self. Although the women in the confessionals locate badness in the self rather than in others or in the social structure, they attempt through confession to rectify their problems, reaffirming their self-worth and their right to be forgiven, to start again, sadder but wiser.

'The lesson I learned was a hard one, but I am willing to accept it now. Nobody is strong enough to control his world . . . But if you share with someone nothing can take it from you' (*True Story*, Romance Special, 1979; p. 116).

The problem with this genre of literature is that it does not allow for personal or social growth. As we indicated earlier, there is no challenge to the self or to the social order through the 'plea'. Rather, the confessions involve an acceptance of the status quo, and an unquestioning assumption of individual responsibility for wrongdoing or wrongthinking. The aim of the confessions is solely restoration without thought of change. Women in the confessionals can only respond to the prevailing social structure, the authority for which rests in the hands of men.

However, if the tragedy of women is found in their separation from the world of social action and public accountability where instrumental modes of expression prevail, the tragedy of men lies in their affective poverty, their inability to respond to situations with feeling or sympathy.

'When I got home (following an attempt at suicide) Mom met me with open arms. Dad stood awkwardly in the doorway, hesitant, not knowing how to handle the situation. I looked at him and smiled. "Hi, Dad. It's good to be home." He fumbled with his tie and said something about how many cookies the children ate . . .' (*True Story*, November 1978; p. 80).

While the socialization of girls stresses affective learning, the socialization of boys puts great stress on early identification with masculine figures, role models, who in order to wield power effectively must be able to present an image of coolness, detachment and rationality. Male heroic figures are generally presented as cold, inarticulate men, men who, when called upon, can make decisions about human lives indifferent to emotional pleas (epitomized in North America by macho figures such as John Wayne and Clint Eastwood). As Sattel (1976) has indicated, this quality of inexpressiveness 'validates the rightness of one's position' by contributing to the appearance of rationality.

Just as the confessional literature denies the possibility of self-growth through confession, so the tradition of non-affectivity denies emotional growth by forbidding the expression of emotions such as tenderness or fear, and by teaching the artificial use of expression to control or manage situations of interpersonal contact where normative behavior demands emotional input.

Confession requires self-revelation. To confess means to lose control, to risk rejection. Men learn not so much to admit as they learn not to confess, thus maintaining control even in the worst situations.

BEYOND THE PLEA: THERAPY AND CONSCIOUSNESS-RAISING

The ability to confess, as we have already indicated, creates the potential for self-development, a potential that as we have seen is not realized in either admission or the confessional 'plea' found in the confessional magazines. To a greater extent however, it is realized in both the therapeutic model and in consciousness-raising, two models of confession which we shall turn to.

The therapeutic model of confession is found as we noted earlier most characteristically in psychiatric or counselling relationships. The client with the help of the therapist probes the motivation behind certain attitudes or behaviors with a view to arriving at insights about the self and repressed experiences. In the trusting therapeutic setting, the client may confess feelings, attitudes and acts that would not or could not be told to others; the patient who is paralyzed can move; the one who reacts hysterically to animals can again walk down a street. Ideally, both the confessee and the therapist agree on the goals of the therapy and the confessions are made only to bring about a conscious realization of one's internal motivations and desires. Unlike the religious confession which is mandatory, the therapeutic confession is volitional; unlike the religious confession which covers a specific list of sins, the therapeutic confession concerns those areas where the patient feels guilt or anxiety. Thus the confessional experience is more individualized and may lead to radical transformations of self-perception and behavior, but it does not lead to any greater analysis of the social structure. Rather, both therapist and patient hope that the client can change herself to fit the world. Thus a young woman learns under the tutelage of her psychiatrist to accept herself for what she 'is':

'That took a lot of doing and in terms of time took another year and a half, but I finally learned to accept the fact that I was a bright but quite ordinary young woman, somewhat passive and shy who was equipped with powerful feminine drives—which simply meant that I badly wanted a husband and children and a happy home' (Kaufman, 1967; p. 25).

Consciousness-raising involves confession of a different quality. Its motives are political—to achieve a radical transformation of the self through a changed perception of social reality. While therapy may temporarily help the individual to become more confident, even to see herself as 'better' than others (Kopinak, 1975), consciousness-raising encourages the development of a critical understanding that personal problems are the result of women's position in the social structure (Kopinak, 1975). This understanding comes about in consciousness-raising through group confessions where the therapist is replaced by the peer group. In the group, formerly private, shameful or anger-provoking experiences become recognized as part of women's collective experience. The difference between this realization and the deprivation of experience found through the confession magazines is that consciousness-raising implies the development of political theory based on the experience of the prevailing social order as oppressive (Bartky, 1977). Victimization is taken beyond the lament of the inevitable found in the confessional magazines to a realization that women are structurally oppressed and that this oppression is an offense. As Kopinak says:

'The explosive element of consciousness-raising is that it introduces the possibility of choice into a situation which was formerly assumed to be by nature static' (Kopinak,

While the consciousness-raising confession holds the greatest potential for self-development of the three confessional models presented, it too has its dangers. There is a temptation with this form of confession, as with all forms, to substitute means for ends. The sheer release of speaking previously deeply hidden thoughts, or sharing formerly unshareable feelings may be substituted for action-oriented strategies. Thus even within the collective atmosphere or the group, individualism may remain supreme, content with structure as long as group support is maintained.

Today, more men are joining women in taking part in consciousness-raising groups, learning to re-interpret their positions in the social structure. But consciousness-raising can only be viewed as an intermediate step. Beyond the confessional lies the task of developing the tools and strategies to effect structural changes. These changes will only occur when both men and women share equally their affective and instrumental worlds, when he can confess and she admit.

REFERENCES

Bardwick, Judith and Douvan, Elizabeth. 1971. Ambivalence: The socialization of woman. In: Gornick, V. and Moran, B. eds, *Woman in Sexist Society*. Basic Books, New York.

Bartky, Sandra, Lee. 1977. Toward a phenomenology of feminist consciousness. In: Vetterling-Braggin, Mary, Elliston, Frederick and English, Jane, eds, *Feminism and Philosophy*. Littlefield Adams, Totowa.

Campbell, Bebe, Moore. November 1978. Hooked on soaps, *Essence*. **9** (7), 100–103.

Dean, John. 1977. *Blind Ambition*. Pocket Books, New York.

Kaufman, Sue. 1967. *Diary of a Mad Housewife*. Random House, New York.

Kincaid, Marylou Butler. 1977. Changes in sex-role attitudes and self actualization of adult woman following a consciousness raising group. *Sex Roles* **3** (4), 329–336.

Kopinak, Kathryn. March 1975. Consciousness raising in the women's movement as political socialization. Unpublished paper, York University.

Lakoff, Robin. 1975. *Language and Woman's Place*. Harper and Row, New York.

Real Confessions, **24** (1) (February 1979).

Sattel, Jack. April 1976. The inexpressive male: tragedy or sexual politics? *Social Problems* **23** (4), 469–478.

True Confessions, December, 1977.

True Story, **119** (4) (November 1978).

True Story, **117** (6) (January 1978).

True Story, **120** (2) (March 1979).

True Story, Spring Romance Special (Spring 1979).

Valian, Virginia. 1977. Linguistics and feminism. In: Vetterling-Braggin, Mary, Elliston, Frederick, English, Jane, eds, *Feminism and Philosophy*. Littlefield Adams, Totowa.

Weibel, Kathryn. 1977. *Mirror Mirror. Images of Women Reflected in Popular Culture*. Anchor Press/ Doubleday, Garden City.

Women's Studies Int. Quart., 1980, Vol. 3. pp. 115–119
© Pergamon Press Ltd.   Printed in Great Britain

0148-0685/80/0301-0115/$02.00/0

REPORT ON THE FIRST NORDIC WOMEN'S PRIZE IN LITERATURE

NANCY COLEMAN

Damvegen 29, N-2380 Brumunddal, Norway

(*Accepted September* 1979)

Since 1962 the Nordic Council has awarded each year a prize in literature to a writer in one of its member nations (Denmark, Finland, Iceland, Norway, Sweden). Each country selects two candidates, and the award is decided by a jury of 10 men (this is meant literally, since only one woman has ever sat on it). The prize is a coveted one. It gives a great deal of prestige to the winner and is usually a guarantee that the author's works will be translated into the other Scandinavian languages and spread to an international audience. Since its founding, however, the prize has never been awarded to a woman, despite the fact that a number of women who are considered leading authors in their own countries, and often have been internationally known, such as Karen Blixen, Tove Ditlevsen, Sara Lidman, Torbjörg Nedreaas, Björg Vik and Svava Jakobsdóttir, have been among the candidates.

At the second annual Research Conference on Women and Literature at Dröbak, Norway in January of this year, it was decided to take action which would make both the reading public and the literary establishment aware of this fact, and ultimately help create an awareness that the work of women writers, although it often is concerned with other spheres of experience and problem areas than that of men, is important literature. Thus the Nordic Women's Prize in Literature was born, and it was decided to award the prize to the Finnish author Märta Tikkanen.*

The award was announced simultaneously with the announcement of the winner of the Nordic Council prize. The 26 women at the conference, among whom were representatives from all the Nordic countries except Finland, decided to go out to the reading public to collect money for the award, which was to be presented on February 20th. Despite the fact that there was only one month in which to collect money, the response was overwhelming. A sum of Nkr. 65,000 (*ca* £6500) was collected, which almost equalled the Dkr. 75,000 (*ca* £7500) from tax funds which were awarded to the winner of the Nordic Council prize. Most donations were small sums given by private persons.

Märta Tikkanen was selected for her poetry collection, *Århundradets Kärlekssaga* (*The Love Story of the Century*), published in 1978. The poems are concerned with the problems she has had combining the roles of wife, mother of four, and professional woman,

---

* *Män Kan Inte Våldtas* by Märta Tikkanen is translated into: Yugoslav (publisher: Izdavacko Poduzéce Otokar Kersovani Rijeka, title: *Muskarce se ne moze silovati*), English (publisher: Virago, title: *Manrape*; Corgi, title: *Manrape*), Danish (publisher: Linhardt og Ringhof Forlag), Norwegian (publisher: Gyldendal), German (publisher: Rowohlt Taschenbuch Verlag), American (publisher: Academy Chicago, Ltd.), Greek (publisher: Women's Publishing Group, Athen).

Århundradets Kärlekssaga by Märta Tikkanen is translated into: Dutch (publisher: Meulenhoff, title: *Het liefdes verhaal van de eeuw*), Danish (publisher: Linhardt og Ringhof Forlag), Norwegian (publisher: Gyldendal).

of how love has been used to suppress her own development, while it probably has nurtured that of her husband, and how love *can* be a positive force.

> I love you so intensely
> you said
> no one has ever been capable of loving as I do
> I have built a pyramid out of my love
> you said
> I have placed you on a pedestal
> high above the clouds
> This is the love story of the century
> you said
> It will last forever
> it will be admired in eternity
> you said
>
> For me it was hard to sleep
> the first seven hundred and thirty nights
> then I realized
> how intensely you love
> your love

Tikkanen's husband, Henrik, is a well-known artist, author, journalist—and a chronic alcoholic. The first section concerns the problems of living with an alcoholic and trying to make some semblance of family life:

> Children
> are not usually the ones
> who take the responsibility when something happens
> At our house
> the seven-year-old took the wine bottle
> hid it half-full behind his back from the police
> once when you were driving under the influence

Henrik Tikkanen has also written about his alcoholism in his autobiography and in his play *Drunken Dog*, so the book is a long shot from being a publicity-hungry way of getting revenge. The wife's version, however, brings out aspects of which neither the public nor the alcoholics themselves are usually made aware:

> Such an honest depiction
> of alcoholism
> say the smart men in the book review section
>
> How come
> none of them
> miss
> for one thing the smells?
> (. . .)

Or what about the way outsiders gossip about the wife of an alcoholic, often condemning
her as the cause of his problem:

If she understands and understands
and forgives
and paves the way
and keeps the relatives at a distance
and keeps the children quiet
and admires
and comforts
and believes and believes and believes
and hopes

then she is an egotistical snob
who is always so damned perfect
and exceptional
an almighty
who thinks she can move mountains
and forgive sins
(. . .)

And if she prays and pleads
and hides bottles
and pours half the contents out the window
and into flowerpots
and dares to lie to the relatives
and blames it on another case of the flu
to his colleagues
and turns a deaf ear
for the 590th time
about his unhappy childhood
and the war he can't forget
and the jealous colleagues

then she's dangerous
conniving and revengeful
(. . .)

And if at last she realizes
that she has her own life
to live
and that someone else's
she can never live
and never bear another's burdens
not even if she wanted to
ever so much
(. . .)

> then she's a hardhearted fiend
> a Goddamn career-seeker
> and throws herself into anything
> and at anyone
> except the person who is closest to her
> and who needs her most
> (. . .)

Many of the poems echo the bitterness we find here, and we wonder, as she asks in the first poem, why she hasn't left her husband. We can gain some insight into the strength of their relationship in Henrik Tikkanen's reaction after reading the manuscript: he said that he would never forgive her if she *didn't* publish the book.

In the second section of the book Tikkanen takes up the theme of love, revealing how the institutions built around love can make the woman experience anything but love and looking for ways to make love work:

> Keep your roses
> clear off the table
> instead
>
> keep your roses
> tell fewer lies
> instead
>
> keep your roses
> listen to what I say
> instead
>
> love me less
> believe in me more
>
> Keep your roses!

In a third group of poems Tikkanen explores the community of women living in love-relationships with men, striving to make the relationships work and also to attain their own goals outside the home. She turns back the pages of her own family history to her great-grandmother, married to a government minister, who wrote secretly at night and whose diary was too risqué to be published, and to her own mother who had to hold her typewriter in her lap when she wrote, while the rest of the family had a desk at which to work.

In all the Scandinavian countries literature written by women has gone through an exciting development in recent years, and Tikkanen's work is symptomatic of much of this. Her first two novels, *Tomorrow* (1970) and *No-man's-land* (1972), are about a woman in crisis because of her desire to be involved in projects outside the home and her fear that her husband won't tolerate such an independent wife. *Who Cares about Doris Mihalov?* (1974) is about an unwed mother. *Men Can't Be Raped* (1975) concerns a woman who gets raped, and after a long reflective process on the use and misuse of violence, decides to take revenge.

A play written for the Stockholm School Theatre in 1979, *Violent Love*, takes up a related theme involving teenagers and the expression of feelings.

Like a number of her sisters in Scandinavia and other countries, Tikkanen has dared to take up themes previously considered taboo or too private to be of interest, and she has used the genre of 'confessional' literature to create literature of quality. In a letter to the Dröbak Group, she said:

'I would like to believe that my book of poetry has become the symbol for all Scandinavian women writers. That is something of which I am very proud. I would never in my wildest thoughts have imagined anything like this during all the nights and days while the lines were being formed. It never was going to be any book, no one would ever read any of it as long as I lived. I thought then.'

Tikkanen plans to use the prize money to publish an anthology of love poems by Finnish women authors, using a system of dual texts, the poems appearing in either the Finnish or Swedish original and in translation to the other of the two languages.

The future of the Nordic Women's Prize is uncertain. Critics of the prize have pointed out that it is equally discriminatory to award a prize just to a woman. This would be the case if there weren't so many processes at work in the Scandinavian literary establishment which eliminate the work of women authors from the system which builds up the reputation of an author. The most influential positions in publishing houses, universities, mass media, etc. are held by men. Men and women still have quite different roles and status in society as a whole, and consequently they have different attitudes to what is important. And the work of women authors is often overlooked or considered trivial by the people who decide what is to be published, reviewed, included in anthologies and literary histories, used in course work in schools and universities, translated—and awarded prizes. In addition women make their literary debut later than the average male author and they usually have less self-confidence. In this sense the Nordic Women's Prize can play an important role, not only in helping to change the system, but also in encouraging women writers and making them 'visible' to the reading public.

At present there are no plans to make the prize an annual award. The Dröbak Group hopes this will be unnecessary. If it were to become annual, one adverse effect might be to further isolate women and their work from the literary establishment, since they then would have 'a prize of their own'. Märta Tikkanen predicts that it will take two years before the official prize will go to a woman, since next year would be 'too obvious'. But there has already been one positive development: Jorunn Hareide, a member of the Dröbak Group, has been appointed to the Norwegian jury.

Women's Studies Int. Quart., 1980, Vol. 3, pp 121–122
Pergamon Press Ltd.   Printed in Great Britain

REPORT ON FEMINIST FILM EVENT

1979 FEMINISM AND CINEMA EVENT

EDINBURGH INTERNATIONAL FILM FESTIVAL

The Feminism and Cinema event was an attempt at the integration and interrogation of feminist film theory and practice. The event's organizers, Laura Mulvey, Claire Johnston, Lynda Myles and Angela Martin, should be complimented for the week-long event which brought together women from all over the world: Great Britain, France, the United States and Canada, Germany, Belgium, Italy and Australia. Days were spent hearing papers, attending workshops and small discussion groups and viewing films. Presentation topics ranged from The Point of Expression in Avant-Garde Film, by Pam Cook; Feminism, Film and the Avant-Garde, by Laura Mulvey; The Subject of Feminist Film, Theory/Practice, by Claire Johnston; Recent Developments in Feminist Criticism, by Christine Gledhill and The Crisis in Naming in Feminist Film Criticism by B. Ruby Rich. As well, there was a forum on feminist film criticism, dealing with the work of various journals (including *Camera Obscura, Jump Cut, M/F, Frauen und Film*) and a forum on feminist film-making practice, conducted by British film-makers.

Overall the event was exceptional, providing for the circulation and discussion of films and ideas. Questions of sexual difference, the production of identification and pleasure in film, the relationship between film text and spectator, a divided subject, film as a social and historical practice, the location of the subject in language—were raised as an integral part of the theoretical discourse of the conference.

The format of the event, however, presented some problems. The schedule was extremely packed, and often one activity conflicted with another. It was difficult to attend film screenings while participating in all other aspects of the conference (e.g. the late afternoon workshops—added to provide extra screenings and discussion time—ran in conflict with other film showings.)

At the same time, we felt, the films screened demanded a more rigorous and specific method of analysis. Often one or two films were cited for accessibility and some cinematic investigation, whereas other films were left entirely undiscussed. Two films which seemed to merit more critical attention were *Invisible Adversaries* by Valie Export and Lis Rhode's *Light Reading*. Both raise problems of representation, repetition and the questioning of traditional narrative structure. Given the fact of a major retrospective, much more analytic attention could have been paid to the work of Chantal Akerman, e.g. investigating problems of family, the home, language of the cinema, and the voice of woman within her films. Although it was discussed considerably, we would also like to mention *Taking Apart* by Jan Worth. The film-maker attempts to examine prostitution as well as its own processes of production.

Because most of the papers dealt with film theory as exceeded by, informed by practice (and we assume the opposite as well), we thought there needed to be a more strenuous application of theoretical ideas to the films shown. And, whereas the papers seemed to call for an avant-garde film practice for feminist cinema, films actually involved in questioning their own forms of representation within an avant-garde context, were not systematically examined. There seemed no means, no language for the discussion of experimental work which was not somehow more easily apprehensible.

If during the feminist event, film theory had truly been integrated with practice, then perhaps the ostensible split between film theoreticians and film-makers, a tension reiterated throughout the 5 days of the conference, might have been alleviated. The very idea of proving the relevance of *theoretical practice* seems odd at this point. Perhaps a definition of theory was needed. For us theory is not just the 'of course' in film practice, but it is a discipline, as is film-making, a rigorous process of analysis, scholarly labor and research. Complaints were raised about difficult language. If one is involved in cinematic work, it seems there would be an obligation, an investment to be made in learning the language, a new tool. However purposely obscure language should be questioned, but difficult terms can be coped with. There was certain resistance to psychoanalysis and semiotics being used as the methodology—the tools—of feminist film theory. Whereas psychoanalysis and semiotics do not provide the only means of decoding film, for us, as film-makers and film theorists, they are major concepts in approaching cinematic structures. We are interested in the practice of film as a radical agent in the transformation of codes. We feel that form should push against, strain the limits of, (cinematic) content.

Another issue discussed each day of the Feminism and Cinema event was the presence of men in the small seminar groups. Because no all-women's study group was established initially, some women formed a women-only discussion group—an act which caused their separation and marginalization from the other participants. The full group could never quite formulate a resolution to the problem and more time was spent discussing the issue than it deserved. (Perhaps some women-only groups should have been set up during the planning of the conference. Eventually each group decided amongst themselves how to deal with the question of male presence.) As one conference participant observed, forcing some women outside the established structure created a situation of sexual difference which duplicated the ways in which women are marginalized and fragmented from the larger society.

In challenging the voice, the authority of the conference, the women's group raised an important question: is the concept of marginality one we, as feminist film-makers and theoreticians, want to preserve? (A question posed also in Claire Johnston's presentation.) We also wonder if it is possible to be anything but marginal? If retaining marginality is desired, then our means of preservation demand that we use our women's discourse—be it a heterogeneous, fragmented discourse—precisely to push against, to force, to challenge patriarchal structures. Differences need to be identified, not abolished. Separatism alone does not problematize patriarchal discourse, but rather allows it to exist unchallenged. On the one hand, it seems important to publicize, to demystify women's private experience, to name those aspects of our lives which have gone too long unnamed. But the forms of those images and representations in film must also be considered.

It is precisely the acceptance of the division between form and content which closes off any possibility of intervention in representation.

Recently we attended a feminist conference at New York University; The Second Sex—Thirty Years Later. Again we found some of the same problems—the ambivalent use of the word 'theory' as the major problem. Whereas language itself, its difficulty, was not an issue, the question of a woman's language, a woman's culture was constantly reiterated. We are struck by the heterogeneity of feminist thought—the different contexts out of which feminism evolved. The success of the Edinburgh event is that it located, within a theoretical framework, the plurality of feminist positions.

The importance of cinema is that it employs the multiplicity of codes at work in the society at large, as well as engaging the spectator in a reciprocity involving the production of meaning. And cinema locates very specifically the problems of women in culture, attendant upon the mode of their representation on the screen. The work that has been done in film theory and film-making is absolutely essential to the continued investigation of feminism through the very opening up, unfixing of those cinematic codes. The Feminism and Cinema event at Edinburgh provided the structure for this sort of feminist discourse.

BETTE GORDON
KARYN KAY

Women's Studies Int. Quart., 1980, Vol. 3, pp. 123–133
Pergamon Press Ltd.   Printed in Great Britain

BOOK REVIEWS

THE PASSIONATE PERILS OF PUBLISHING, 76 pages. Booklegger, San Francisco. Price U.S. $5.00.

Librarians have always been cognizant of the intrepid *Booklegger*, a California-based periodical, published from 1972 by feminist librarians and full of annotated bibliographies and information from the small presses on such alternative issues as menstruation, self-defence, and holistic health. Now all have a chance to sample Booklegger's fare, in their latest 'sporadical', *The Passionate Perils of Publishing*, on the fast-growing alternative to big business—self-publishing. *PPP* opens with the incredible but true facts on conglomerates in the publishing world ('3·3 per cent of 6000 plus publishing companies control 70 per cent of the industry's volume'). As this literary–industrial complex is controlled by rich, white hetero males, what are feminist writers to do? 'Roll yr own', is the advice from Booklegger and proceeds to detail the process of self-publishing from beginning to end, not forgetting distribution. For this whole process, Booklegger provides wide-ranging and up-to-date annotated bibliographies on alternative and feminist publishing including guides, directories, indexes, distributors, presses, periodicals and review media 'interspiced' with surrealistic graphics.

The Passionate Perils ends with an annotated list of library periodicals and newsletters (many alternative) such as the *Women Library Workers' directory* of feminist library workers in the United States and Canada. This directory lists such pertinent information as who's into what and who's good for a crash space or cup of coffee.

On the 'fervid fuschia' back cover, Celeste West and Valerie Wheat, the illustrious writer-publishers of this venture, detail for all future self-publishers the actual cost figures of the *PPP* itself, including items often forgotten such as the 100 free review copies. A super bonus to this 76-page information-filled marvel.

Celeste West, the entrepreneur of *Booklegger*, began as a San Francisco librarian-editor of *Synergy*, an alternative magazine born of the 60s political atmosphere, that functioned as a current awareness of the American independent press for librarians. As the 60s ferment died down the California state librarian ordered Celeste to 'stop the presses'. Celeste, after more or less futile fighting, decided to 'roll her own' and thus Booklegger publishing was born.

The first production, in 1972, aptly named *Revolting Librarian Rides Again*, was written, typed and distributed out of Celeste's home. Sixteen fact-filled issues followed, plus two irreplaceable guides—*Women's Films in Print* by Bonnie Dawson and *Positive Images: Non-Sexist Films for Young People.* by Susan Wengraf and Linda Artel and now the latest Booklegger production, *The Passionate Perils of Publishing*.

Though hampered by no investment capital, a continuing need to promote and distribute out of her home (which means a basement constantly filled with books) and a minimal survival income, Celeste West in her indomitable enthusiasm for self-publishing is even now planning future issues on 'anarchy–feminism' and 'creative erotica' (complete with photos!) She and all the Bookleggers need and deserve feminists' encouragement and support for this strong, alternative voice in publishing.

Past issues of *Booklegger*, the two guides mentioned above and *The Passionate Perils of Publishing* can all be ordered from Booklegger, 555–29th Street, San Francisco, CA 94131, U.S.A.

JACQUELYN MARIE
Publisher of *Wild Iris Journal, Woman Library Worker*

STARS by Richard Dyer, 204 pages. British Film Institute,* 1979. Price £2.45 inc. p & p.

Stars is a book about heavenly bodies; not the astrological type, but the cinematic variety at which we continue to gaze in awe and wonder, paying the entrance fee to the darkened chamber for the sheer pleasure of looking at them. The pun, and the idea of magic and mystery on which it is based, is far from irrelevant to the phenomenon of Hollywood's star-system and the cinematic institution it supports. The book recognizes

---

* Study material of particular interest to Women's Studies courses available from the Educational Advisory Service, British Film Institute, 81 Dean St., London W1V 6AA, U.K.

Teacher's Study Guide 1: *The Stars* by Richard Dyer. Price £0.90 (inc. p & p); *The Dumb Blonde Stereotype* by Richard Dyer. Price £0.90 (inc. p & p); *Women's Film List*. Price £0.90 (inc. p & p).

BFI. Book Library bibliography No. 51: *Women and the Cinema*, free from BFI.

Gays and Film edited by Richard Dyer. Price £1.65 (inc. p & p).

Women in Film Noir edited by E. Ann Kaplan. Price £1.95 (inc. p & p).

the analogy, tries to account for the phenomenon, to put a critical distance between us and our experience of it, and rather ambiguously finishes by closing the gap, reasserting the author's wish to retain those moments of identification and fascination into which stars seduce us. Intended primarily as a teaching aid, it provides a comprehensive survey of existing material on the star-system, its social and cinematic function and effects, with detailed analyses of specific star images.

The book is published by the Educational Advisory Service of the British Film Institute as part of an ongoing project of providing film study materials on all aspects of the cinema, including women and film. At a time when feminist study of the Hollywood star-system is only beginning (although a mass of material from every other conceivable standpoint already exists) a book which approaches the subject seriously from the point of view of sexual politics is very welcome. The 11-page bibliography, which includes several pieces of gay and feminist film criticism, is an achievement in itself, although some annotation would have helped to distinguish between the overwhelming variety of approaches.

Part One starts from the assumption that stars, like cinema itself, perform an ideological function in bourgeois society, and are produced and consumed through language, i.e. through the discourses of publicity, fan magazines and film criticism as well as through films themselves. Dyer summarizes various sociological and phenomenological approaches to the questions: why do we need/get stars, and why do we need/get the stars we do, and the informational content of these summaries, and others throughout the book, is very valuable. I missed any analysis from Dyer of the methodological differences of approach, sometimes profoundly contradictory, for instance between the transparent sociological approach and more sophisticated arguments which see stars as performing some kind of symbolic function in society, thus raising the problem of language. Without an analytical overview of the way stars function as part of the cinematic institution, and the place of that institution in bourgeois patriarchal society, it is hard to accept Dyer's description of ideology as contradictory as anything more than a rationalization for the central argument of the book: the subversive potential of star 'charisma'. The word is not intended in its popular sense: it is appropriated from the political theory of Max Weber and used to mean the way in which a number of contradictory elements are held together in one extraordinary individual, with whom we then identify. Thus Douglas Fairbanks combined and reinforced a number of ideas which went with the idea of 'being a good American' at a time in American history (1940) when those ideas were in jeopardy, and Marilyn Monroe's 'combina ion of sexuality and innocence', part of the flux of sexual mores in American society, made her 'seem to "be" the very tensions that ran through the ideological life of fifties America'. However, identification with a male hero who overcomes contradiction is very different from identification with a woman at whose expense and across whose body the contradictions are resolved. The contradiction for feminists here is one between the exploitation of the female figure on which the star-system and narrative cinema rests, and our pleasure in the formal beauty of the fetish figure.

Richard Dyer is writing from his position in the gay movement, which has always taken pleasure in Hollywood's charismatic stars as signs of sexual ambiguity, offering a distance on 'normal' heterosexuality. While it's clear that rejection of these stereotypes based on puritanism is non-productive, real problems remain with any argument which gives stereotypes a positive value in themselves outside the ordering of sexual difference in patriarchal society. Richard Dyer seems to accept normative definitions of heterosexuality as non-contradictory, in straight opposition to homosexuality (p. 66) which leads him to suggest that there is something in the homosexual point of view which privileges it in relation to heterosexuality. Secondly, while Hollywood's fetish figures have traditionally offered a kind of subversive pleasure to both homosexuals and heterosexuals, the strength of these figures is more apparent than real, and they cannot be seen as transcending the oppressive forms of dominant language, which locates the woman's body as the site of the playing out of male anxieties.

Part Two concentrates on those forms of discourse outside film which contribute to the building of star images, laying out the arguments in impressive detail and including material, like fan-magazines, often regarded as too trivial for serious study. These surrounding discourses act as an anchorage for the image of the star as a 'real person', providing a coherence which overlays the contradictory sign-clusters of stars as they appear in different films as different characters. Dyer discusses some of the 'social types' to which stars correspond: the good guy, the tough guy, the pin-up, the rebel hero and the independent woman, suggesting their subversive potential, and the chapter includes a detailed account of the building of one star image: Jane Fonda. The account forms a fascinating narrative, a 'family romance' in which Jane Fonda goes through a crisis of sexual identity in her struggle to become an 'independent person'. In contrast to Dyer's account, I would argue that the interest of Jane Fonda's image for feminists is not in its apparently 'positive' political character, but in the way it signifies a state of emotional and sexual crisis, underlined by hysteria. Thus the fact that both homosexuals and heterosexuals respond to the image is not hard to understand, since both are constituted as contradictory structures within patriarchal society. What needs to be asked is how capitalism and patriarchy manipulate and recuperate the image and our response to it in their own interests.

Part Three places star images in specific film texts, showing how they are selected to interact with the demands of character and fiction in narrative film, drawing on literary and theatrical theory and extending this to film. The detailed discussion of the construction of character and its relationship to narrative structure produces an argument that characters in bourgeois fiction must be rendered coherent. Obviously stars, whose meaning can change from film to film, derive their coherence from the non-cinematic discourses which create and support the star image, and help us to guess what the character in a fiction might be thinking, an 'interiority' provided by the novel but not by film, except in certain limited ways which Richard Dyer discusses. Most important in this section is the argument about the signifying function of 'performance', which is linked to the idea of 'charisma'. Dyer argues that the gestures and expressions specific to a particular star not only contribute to the meaning of a film, but contribute extra meaning and can work against the intended meaning. The example given is Marilyn Monroe as Lorelei in 'Gentlemen Prefer Blondes'. The argument is that her star image of 'innocent sexuality' does not fit the cynical gold-digging Lorelei of Anita Loos' play, and that this problematic fit creates a gap between star image and character which makes it difficult for the spectator to read the character coherently. This example is problematic in many ways: by concentrating on one aspect of Monroe's image Dyer ignores the process of production of meanings in the film as a whole, suggesting that the image somehow escapes patriarchal ideology. Similarly, while Bette Davis' performance in 'The Little Foxes' certainly signifies a contradiction between 'unnatural desires' and 'natural wife and mother', the unnatural performance works within patriarchal ideology to support Davis' signifying function, in this instance, as 'unnatural woman'. Performance signs, like all signs, are material units of language existing within history and ideology.

However, it is difficult not to feel, with Richard Dyer, that star images do have something extra, an excess of form which threatens to escape the codes of dominant language. *Stars* makes a valuable contribution towards analysing this elusive phenomenon, and the notions of 'self' and 'expression' that go with it, and much of the value of the book lies in the questions it provokes. Recent work by feminists on women and the cinema has begun to pose the problem of representations of sexuality differently, attempting to define sexual structures as contradictory within the general context of the structures of patriarchal ideology and language. Richard Dyer draws on some of this work without pointing to crucial differences of approach. Perhaps the next step is to begin to understand these differences.

PAM COOK

DECODING ADVERTISEMENTS by Judith Williamson, 180 pages. Marion Boyars. Price, hardback £7.95, paperback £3.95.

Although feminists recognize the importance of advertising images, much criticism and strategy has remained at the level of denunciation. *This exploits/degrades women* stickers are an active challenge to 'woman as spectacle' on the hoardings, but demonstrably one that advertisers, with characteristic adaptability, can even turn to advantage. Current debates on women and representation point to the limitations of 'sexism' as a term of blanket condemnation, and drawing on psychoanalytic theory, stress the importance of the structures of representation: the issue is *how* advertisements work.

For many, the terrain of these debates and theories is unfamiliar and mystifying. *Decoding Advertisements* is far from being a simple primer, but, as its title suggests, it is offered as a kind of manual, a set of tools for dismantling and labelling the mechanisms through which advertisements produce meaning and as an exploration of how we ourselves are engaged in that process. The techniques of semiological analysis employed throughout are explained with a clarity the uninitiated will appreciate.

Judith Williamson argues that in addition to their economic function of selling things to us—and at the same time obscuring the process of production and the class differences on which capitalism is based—advertisements also perform the ideological function of creating structures of meaning within which we ourselves become positioned. They appropriate the material basis of social reality and symbolically transform it into myth, providing us with a system of meanings that enable us to make sense of the world. Their referents are what is already there, what is taken for granted, what is assumed as natural. For women the implications of this analysis are crucial: advertisements (and other visual representations) do not distort our social reality but are part of the process of constructing it.

The author's elaboration of her argument is linked with detailed analysis and discussion of the 120 advertisements illustrated. This makes the book immediately accessible and fun, though at another level the breadth of its theoretical approach also makes it demanding reading. It takes its starting point in Marx, advances by way of Althusser's theory of ideology and the category of the subject developed by Lacan and deploys at various stages the work of Levi-Strauss, Barthes, Freud, and others. Structuralist theory is central but Judith Williamson is not uncritical of what she sees as academic structuralism, declaring herself 'impatient with any theory of ideology which is not tied to anything practical, to the material factors which influence our feelings, our lives, our images of ourselves'. She emphasizes that the concepts she uses are tools selected for their particular usefulness. The book opens up a lot of questions. It does not answer all of them and some are barely formulated; it does map out—and very skilfully—directions for further analyses and strategies to be pursued.

LIZ HERON

USING THE MEDIA by Denis MacShane, 215 pages. Pluto Press, London, 1979. Price, hardback £7.95, paperback £2.50.

If you find yourself suddenly asked to take part in a television studio discussion you might leaf through Chap. 9 of this book for advice on what to wear—'Be neat'—what to say and, more importantly, what not to say.

Using the Media is a handbook for 'workers and community activists' which aims to provide in detail practical advice on how to use the media before they use you. The book gives a comprehensive view of the structures and working-processes of the mass media and contains a useful directory of press, radio and television organizations.

Much recent work on the representation of women in the media points to their misrepresentation and some studies venture further to show how the women's movement and important feminist ideas have been incorporated into mainstream journalism, television, cinema, etc. There is an uncomfortable feeling that the women's movement has been 'sold' to the mass audience in ways over which we have little or no control.

The labour movement has already alerted its members to the need to take some responsibility over how they are represented in the mass media. A booklet has recently been published by the Trades Union Congress which offers guidelines to trade unionists on 'How to Handle the Media' stressing that the media are one of the most powerful weapons in society and that: 'It is therefore a weapon which it is better to use than to have used against you.' One way we could start to combat current dominant images of women in the media is to learn how to use—handle—the mass media.

This book covers a vast number of areas including advice on writing and issuing press releases, organizing news conferences, participating in phone-ins and guidelines for dealing with press, radio and television reporters. MacShane offers useful tips to potential television interviewees so they can make 'the most effective presentation of their case.' He outlines in detail the different functions of a television production team and emphasizes the importance of deciding beforehand which points you want to get over. It is important to know your facts, look directly at the interviewer and be ready to challenge her/him and change the parameters of the debate if necessary. For example, a useful technique might be to say: 'I'll come back to that in a moment but what is really important . . .' Such advice is crucial to any feminist invited to speak on say, abortion, where a television discussion is likely to centre on the question of the morality/immorality of the taking of human life. In this situation we need to employ effective strategies in order to redirect the question to a woman's right to choose.

If you are being recorded on film and you feel you are making a complete mess of an answer, MacShane advises that you just come to a stop and ask if you can do it again: 'A trick to make this appear less contrived is to have a major coughing fit, or suddenly swear and then stop in embarrassment. They will have to start again' (p. 147).

MacShane explains the importance of making yourself and your organization known to editors, producers, journalists etc., so that your availability for comment is made apparent: 'Far better than sending off letters and press releases or phoning up newsrooms out of the blue is to have a personal relationship with a journalist who can be approached direct' (p. 110). He does not, however, recognize or deal with the particular situation women face in having to deal with male journalists who often refuse to consider 'women's issues' as newsworthy. MacShane does not feel happy with news values as they stand but he argues that 'for the time being we have to take the media as they are' (p. 2.). For trade unions this means struggling for fairer representation within the existing structures of the media—but what are women to do when they are structurally excluded from the current definition of what constitutes 'news'?

MacShane does not address himself to this problem but instead urges that activists should not forget that although the news pages are of greatest concern, other sections of the paper need a constant flow of ideas and stories too: 'There is no permanently unchanging reason why women's pages should, as in so many cases they do, concentrate on fashion, cookery and household hints. The problems of women at work, the fight for equal pay, etc., can make good feature material for a women's page' (p. 53). Behind this liberal facade MacShane is dutifully adhering to traditional male media practices by refusing to see that news about women's work is as important as news about men's work and their fight for pay.

In his section on magazines, journals and the left press he mentions *Socialist Worker* but not *Women's Voice* and makes no reference to *Spare Rib* or other feminist publications.

This is a book packed with useful information about the structure and professional practices of the British mass media and from that point of view it will serve as a valuable resource book for the women's movement. But it is not enough for the author to use she/he and her/his in the text (with occasional lapses) and at the same time fail totally to recognize the special position of women in relation to the mass media. The book is written for a specific purpose: 'to equip workers, trade union officials, community activists, local political activists and pressure groups for the most effective use of the media' (p. 1). Has Denis MacShane forgotten that all the above categories have women in their ranks?

HELEN BAEHR

HEARTH AND HOME—IMAGES OF WOMEN IN THE MEDIA edited by Gaye Tuchman, Arlene Kaplan Daniels and James Benet, 333 pages. Oxford University Press, Oxford. Price £2.25.

Few readers of this journal will need reminding that the mass media deal in stereotypes—simplified, recognizable images of people carrying messages about how people are and how they should be—nor that women as a social group are either marginally or negatively defined in the media. A book about sex-role stereotypes in the mass media should then be of general interest to feminists and a powerful tool in our struggle to change sexist images for progressive ones.

The book is organized round the themes of the symbolic annihilation and trivialization of women in the mass media. It is divided into four parts, on television, women's magazines, newspapers and women's pages and the effects of television on children and youth. A concluding chapter deals with the policy implications of the material in the book.

The research contained in this book relates mainly to American society and experience. This does not in itself mean that the book is of no relevance to other readers who are concerned with cultural representations of women and women's issues. However two difficulties do arise. One is that the frame of reference and the examples cited might be unfamiliar to the non-American. The second is a more complex argument concerning the nature of social science in American academe. The editors have endeavoured to make this compilation accessible to the general reader—there is very little sociological jargon—but the dominant assumption and strain of American social science is empirical positivism, a strain which has organized mass communication research around concepts of the 'mass', 'effect' and 'function'. European media research on the other hand has directed itself to classical European social thought for inspiration and models, to marxism, structuralism, phenomenology and new types of literary criticism and aesthetics. The latter have shifted from the interpretation of the meaning of media and literary 'texts' to an investigation of the means of production, aesthetic structures and theories of representation and ideology.

In her introduction Gaye Tuchman examines the issues of sex-role stereotyping and its impact on girls and women and 'national life' in the United States. Needless to say the evidence suggests that the media, particularly television, provide unrealistic, trivial and limiting representations of women.

Despite the paucity of research on women and the mass media, Tuchman concludes from her survey of the available material that the media's message to society is that women don't matter much. The evidence she cites is based on experimental and survey-type research as well as content analyses of TV, magazines, etc. She fails to make the necessary and important distinctions between the different methodological approaches or to question the assumptions which lie behind them. In general these research assumptions are behaviouristic, i.e. they argue that behaviour resulting from exposure to, say, the mass media obeys laws of conditioning, reinforcement, dissonance, sublimation or expresses urges or scars such as an inferiority complex. Summing up her introductory survey Tuchman writes,

'Watching a lot of television leads children and adolescents to believe in traditional sex roles: Boys should work, girls should not . . . They teach that women should direct their hearts towards hearth and home' (p. 37).

My unease lies with her uncritical acceptance of the dominant paradigm of mass communications research which makes simplistic, unidirectional and reductive connections between media and behaviour and which neutralises and suppresses the vital question of 'meaning' and the interconnections between different levels of the social formation. Her conclusion does not challenge existing social and economic structures. She suggests that because the media underestimate women's involvement in the labour force and encourage their underachievement, this is economically damaging to the nation as well as to the individual. The assumption seems to be that *numerically* increasing women's participation in the workforce will bring about their liberation. Women's exploitation and subordination is constituted sexually and ideologically but *also* politically and economically. That is why a feminist analysis of culture must harness such conceptual tools as the 'sexual division of labour', the economic relations and relations of reproduction in order to challenge the oppressive economic and ideological status quo.

Most of the articles in the book are of an empirical nature either centring on audience response to sex-typing or on a quantification or discussion of women as they appear in television programmes, in magazines, etc. George Gerbner in his article 'The dynamics of cultural resistance' is one of the few contributors to introduce questions of theory, probing some of the connections between the media's role and the established structure of social relations. He observes the media's current counter-attack on, and recuperation of, the women's movement. He suggests that when women or other groups denied access to power are shown as independent, adventurous and powerful, they are portrayed (on television) as *enforcing* rather than challenging the laws that oppress them (p. 50). They act on behalf of and not against the rules designed to protect the dominant group's interests.

In her discussion of women's magazines in Britain, Margorie Ferguson introduces the notion of ideology as presented on magazine covers. She describes the inherent contradiction of these images of womanhood, both expressing as they do the middle-class world of the middle-class woman and yet also suggesting the idea that class is irrelevant to definitions of femininity. The face of femaleness is the face of the smiling pleaser. Despite the author's definition of the producer's and audience's shared understanding as an oscil‑lating ideology, she mistakes the intimate relationship between magazines and their readers as a causal one. It is not magazines in themselves that determine what women are. Women are constructed outside the media as well, and it is their marginality in culture generally *and* in the media which contributes to their sub-ordinated position.

A useful idea is explored in Carol Lopate's analysis of Jacqueline Kennedy Onassis's treatment in 12 American magazines. Lopate makes the link between women's representation and their economic condition. Jackie is predominantly treated in ways that allow the magazines to project their own aspirations, images and ideology of women, which define work outside the home negatively and associate happiness and emotional fulfillment not with money but with children and the home. 'With this definition, women remain the group that can be pushed in or pulled out of the labour force, depending on the economy's needs' (p. 140).

Some space in the book is also given to production practices and the place of women journalists in these practices and institutions. Gladys Engel Lang's article on 'The most admired woman: image-making in the news' and Tuchman's 'The newspaper as a social movement's resource' are uneven in the quality of their argument and again seem to work within the dominant economic and ideological paradigm.

As an example of the worst type of social scientism and mystification, I would cite G. William Domhoff's 'The women's page as a window on the ruling class'. The author uses, superfluously, a battery of 'scientific' techniques and jargon, computers and statistical analysis, not to mention a reach-me-down style of writing, to tell us some self-evident truism: that there is a ruling class in America. He would have found out the same (and more) by studying the Hearst family business empire, who own the San Francisco Chronicle whose pages he finds so transparently revealing.

Most of the studies included in this collection are based on content analysis. As a method content analysis is an impoverished means of discovering the aesthetic structures and media practices which produce an ideological effect in the material they organize. Content and expressive forms are related in a complex mediation to culture as a lived experience, to configurations of ideas and beliefs in society—connections which are fatally written out of the content analysis paradigm. Content seems to be emptied of interest and significance to these researchers once its relevance to matters of behavioural change has been implied. Little or no attention is given to the theoretical context which determines this kind of research and which locks it into a social status quo. Stereotypes of women will not necessarily vanish on the production of an image of 'real' women. We must look beyond content to forms of culture and social order i.e. to patriarchy, to more general social and economic conditions, to the relations between cultural production and meaning and crucially to a theory of images, to questions of identification, recognition and cultural reading. The themes of this book, the ideas and issues it seeks to investigate are of great concern to feminists and should provide the framework for political action and change. On the whole it is an opportunity missed. This is in large measure due to the inherent conservatism and narrow approach of a school of social science research, which cannot provide the conceptual tools and critical analysis that is demanded of the subject of images in the media. A more critical, even self-critical, approach might have helped us understand how women's subordination is articulated through the media and through social structures.

GILLIAN DYER

WOMEN AND THE NEWS, edited by Laurily Keir Epstein, 144 pages. Communication Arts Books, Hastings House, New York, 1978. Price, hardback U.S. $12.50.

Although it never happened, everybody has heard of the bra-burning incident. This kind of reporting is symptomatic of the Western mass media's attitude to women's news.

Hence I expected this book to have grappled with the urgent problems of women's news coverage, to have mapped out and systematically analyzed the present conflicts between media and feminism and to have indicated the areas which feminist communications could—potentially—most easily penetrate.

However that has not proved to be the case with *Women and the News*. It is an 'outgrowth' of a 1977 Washington University media studies conference—as stressed by the blurb—and I suspect that its academic origins ought to be blamed for the fact that women's media issues are fitted into available mainstream media sociology patterns. Epstein admits that much in her introduction when she says that the aim is to examine three current concepts in news media research—agenda-setting, access to the media and definitions of the news—and their relevance to women's concerns. The resulting assortment of eight contributions written by sociologists and media practitioners of both sexes lacks a consistency of approach and attitude to the media, feminism and 'women's concerns' which are never clearly defined, and seem to mean different things to different authors.

The problems of women's coverage are viewed within a specifically North American context, such as the First Amendment contests, Fairness Doctrine controversies and draw exclusively on U.S. and Canadian printed sources and experience so that their relevance to non-American conditions is greatly circumscribed.

But the book is not a completely wasted opportunity. It has succeeded in presenting in one concise volume a host of questions pertinent to the media's attitude to women's issues and news, something which has not been done before.

American 'media effects' research in the early seventies established that the press (broadcasting to a lesser degree) is not very successful in telling people what to think but has been 'stunningly' successful in telling them what to think *about*, i.e. in setting up the agenda. Graber's study 'Agenda-Setting: Are There Women's Perspectives?', contradicts this function for it shows that women get disproportionately affected by scanty women's news coverage. However, no conclusion is drawn from this discovery of a case of skewed agenda-setting effects, instead, Graber closes her essay with the following statement:

'Once the stereotype of women as political primitives has been laid to rest, the media, ever anxious to supply the interested public with what it wants to read and hear, are bound to give better coverage to issues that are of great concern to their female audiences. If women are perceived as alert to the news and as major contributors to public opinion, the media, as well as the political world, will reflect greater respect for women's political interests and power' (p. 35).

Firstly, despite her own empirical results showing that women's attitude to the general news is not different from that of men, Graber perpetuates the myth of women as 'political primitives' and blames them for the existence of the stereotype whilst totally ignoring the social, political and economic conditions which led to its creation in the first place.

Secondly, Graber's belief in a benevolent media system fulfilling the wishes of 'the interested public' is extremely naïve and a position abandoned even by the staunch supporters of the libertarian theory of press. In short, the media do distinguish between powerful and powerless publics and acceptable and subversive ideas. Graber herself seems to qualify her assumption when saying that the media 'will reflect greater respect' for women's issues if women are perceived as 'major contributors to public opinion' and holders of political power. As such a situation is unlikely to be achieved in the foreseeable future, feminist media sociologists ought to be inquiring whether it is possible to get 'respectable' coverage of women's news *within* the existing press and broadcasting structures, and if not, what needs to be done.

Public right of access to the media has been suggested as one avenue for exploration. In this book, however, access is not understood to mean a way of opening up the media to the 'unrepresented' public in order to provide freer flow of information, i.e. to democratize communications in ways which would lead to a democratization of the whole society. Drawing on the American experience, authors of the relevant essays define access as professional journalists lending their professional ear more readily to unrepresented groups. Eddie Goldenberg describes access as the 'sympathetic or detailed coverage of disadvantagous group's point of view' mediated by a professional. So far all the attempts 'of minorities and women' have failed to achieve constitutional rights of access to the media; ironically, the outcome of all the litigation has been the Supreme Court's emphasis on the journalist's individual 'editorial discretion'.

Mary Ann Yodelis Smith in her 'Access to the Media' asks for a 'consensual' method of access to be devised in future. For the present she complacently advocates:

'Citizen's agreements, reached with broadcasters, and even with the print media, in negotiations outside the courtroom, are a fruitful way to achieve change so long as the First Amendment is cherished' (p. 81).

Despite the fact that all the case histories she examines contradict such an assumption. For the only 'fruitful way' through which women have achieved any concrete and lasting victory has been through the courts by enforcing existing state and federal equal opportunity laws.

For its treatment of the impact of feminism on news the most relevant essay is Gertrude Joch Robinson's 'Women, Media Access and Social Control'. She argues that there have been noticeable changes in the American coverage of women's issues:

'These changes in mode of portrayal from no mention, to sensationalism, to less prestigious portrayal are a result of *changes in professional values and practices* within media as well as changes in public outlooks. Both of these were until recently assumed to be relatively impervious to redefinition' (p. 104).

Robinson believes that media professional values have changed to accommodate feminism. Yet there is a flaw in her argument. She states that the media have 'routinized access to feminist organizations', that their portrayal is selective and issues are trivialized and admits herself that only *some* aims and norms of the movement have been legitimatized. Most acceptable being those which are—according to Robinson—'within the American value structures, such as education and employment equality'. I would argue that the more radical demands and the ultimate one—the abolition of patriarchy—are as unacceptable to the media as they have ever been. It is not professional values and media practices which have been altered but basically 'unchanged media' which have created an acceptable, incorporated type of feminism.

Robinson's second assumption must also be challenged for she seems to imply that:

'Other ways of changing perspectives from which stories are covered is to hire more women into the media professions' (p. 104).

Yet she is unable to demonstrate how the presence of more women reporters has produced any real changes in media attitudes towards women's issues. The only evidence she can point to is superficial adjustment: avoiding sexually stereotyped descriptions of a woman's looks and clothes and not referring to women by their first names only. Robinson does not seem to view professional journalists 'realistically', within the existing constraints of capitalist mass media, where a woman in order to succeed—to paraphrase a current saying—must be twice as professional as a man. But sooner or later her professionalism, i.e. her internalized media practice ethics, is bound to conflict with her feminism because the two are—in their present 'forms'—ideologically incompatible.

This contradiction between professionalism and feminism is the fundamental problem in the relationship of feminism to mainstream professional journalist practice and is in urgent need of examination. It is a pity that this question is not broached at all in this book.

The conflict reappears in a different form when the issue of women's news is problematized. Suzanne Pingree and Robert Hawkins argue that the reason for the bias and absence of women's news is to be found in the professional criterion of newsworthiness. What feminists would like to communicate is not considered a real event-news by media professionals who have been professionally conditioned to supply 'objective', fair and balanced news products which allow no space for issue-news aimed at either explanation or persuasion. At the same time, as the authors point out, in existing political, economic and social conditions women are excluded from positions from which they could initiate event-news. Their conclusion is rather pessimistic:

'Until women are no longer discriminated against in society as a whole, they will continue to face an uphill battle to put themselves and their issues before the general public' (p. 133).

Leon Sigal in 'Defining News Organizationally: News Definitions in Practice', having examined present media practices, states that feminist news can be accommodated only 'in those corners of the newsroom that are relatively less restricted by beats and routine channels', i.e. on the women's page. Like other contributors who touch on this issue Sigal believes that change must first happen in society at large. Implicitly, he refuses to consider whether news can play any part in bringing about change. Whilst Sigal's discouraging conclusion is persuasively argued, it is one which ought to be theoretically and practically challenged by feminists. *Women and the News* does not take up this challenge.

ANGELA SPINDLER-BROWN

WOMEN IN FILM NOIR edited by E. Ann Kaplan, 129 pages. British Film Institute. Price, paperback £1.50.

Feminism has most frequently criticized mainstream cinema in terms of its 'stereotypical' and 'unrealistic' portrayal of women. This approach, however, has been called into question by Hollywood's recently demonstrated ability to deal 'realistically' (in films such as *Alice doesn't live here anymore, An unmarried woman, Klute* etc.) with the so-called 'new independent woman' without, nevertheless, jettisoning traditional patriarchal values. The development of a feminist film criticism has thus now become vital not simply for feminists within the academic discipline of film studies but for all women seeking to challenge the ways in which patriarchal capitalism seeks to incorporate our struggle.

The collection of essays in *Women in Film Noir* together make a constructive contribution to this task. The term *film noir* refers to a group of films produced between around 1941 and 1958, mostly 'B' feature thrillers, which have in common labyrinthine plot structures, a highly elaborated visual style and, as their stock characters, hard-boiled heroes and, most interestingly, *femmes fatales*. The woman of *film noir*, unlike her innocent sister in the 'A' films of the period, was a woman who used her sexuality as a weapon of power over men and so could participate actively in the film narrative. In these films, as E. Ann Kaplan points out, 'Although the man is sometimes simply destroyed because he cannot resist the woman's lures . . . often the work of the film is the attempted restoration of order through the exposure and then destruction of the sexual, manipulating woman'. *Film noir* is interesting for feminists not only because they take women's sexuality as a central concern but also, as Sylvia Harvey points out in her essay, because the family and stable family relations, are conspicuously absent in these films.

Significantly, these films were produced over a period which saw rapid changes in the position of women in American society. The Second World War, which brought increased economic and sexual independence for women, followed after the war by unemployment and attempts by capital to 'encourage' women back into the home—all these factors combined to throw the traditional ideology of women's place into crisis. Several of the essays in this volume attempt to trace the relations between the films and contemporary social conditions. Although—as the authors would doubtless be the first to admit—these attempts are somewhat sketchy, they open up an important area of future work on the factors modifying the representation of women within bourgeois cultural production.

The central concern of all these essays is to clarify the attitude a feminist film practice should take to the conventions and stereotypes of *film noir*. In a valuable theoretical contribution, Christine Gledhill criticizes feminists' frequent rejection of genre films as 'unrealistic' in their portrayal of women, and argues that in fact the formalized and foregrounded sets of codes used by *film noir* enable feminist criticism to produce 'progressive' readings of many of these films. She develops the important notion of the 'woman's discourse' that is to be heard at certain points within film narrative where the dominant male discourse loses control, challenging the latter's assumptions about women.

Such a woman's discourse is identified by E. Ann Kaplan in Fritz Lang's film *The Blue Gardenia;* through it, she argues, the film is able to show that the notion of the *femme fatale* is a product of male discourse sustained only to the extent that patriarchy can suppress the voice of women. Kaplan's article raises the question of the extent to which a film produced within capitalist patriarchy can 'expose' the position of women within that system. In his article on *Gilda*, Richard Dyer shows that the film is progressive in that the central woman figure is constructed as knowable and 'normal' as against the 'inadequate' film hero, but that this construction relies on conventional notions of 'adequacy' and 'masculinity'. Gilda can appear 'normal' only because Johnny is implied to be homosexual.

Janey Place in her article locates the radical effect of *film noir* in its conflict between narrative structure and visual style. While the progress of the narrative is usually towards the destruction of the *femme fatale*, visually the woman is given 'such freedom of movement and dominance that it is her strength and sensual visual texture that is inevitably printed in our memory, not her ultimate destruction'.

Two other articles examine these films in terms of specific theories of women's oppression. Claire Johnston contributes a Lacanian reading of the key *noir* film *Double Indemnity*, while Pam Cook draws on the theories of Freud and Bachofen in her discussion of *Mildred Pierce*. Both articles seem to me rather unproductive in treating the films only as exemplifications of theories from elsewhere and thus tending to obscure the points at which *film noir*, through its own procedures for producing meaning, may reveal the contradictions of its patriarchal project.

This reservation notwithstanding, *Women in Film Noir* makes an important contribution to the feminist intervention in film culture. Even though some differences in approach between the contributors are not perhaps drawn out sufficiently, this valuable collection of essays should stimulate further important work. An added bonus is the fascinating collection of frame enlargements, which strikingly illustrate Janey Place's thesis that *film noir* is the only period in American film in which women are 'deadly but sexy, exciting and strong'.

PAT HARPER

CATALOGUE OF BRITISH FILM INSTITUTE PRODUCTIONS 1977–78, edited by Elizabeth Cowie, 94 pages. Available from British Film Institute, 127 Charing Cross Rd, London, W.C.2. Price £1.50.

This catalogue presents the films and video-tapes funded by the BFI Production Board from 1976 to 1978. '*Presents*' is here a key term, since only 15 films are catalogued in a book of over 90 pages. Five of the films had women directors and one of these (*Rapunzel*) was jointly directed by women. The catalogue is much more than a list of films available, of hire costs and running times. It is 'an attempt to explore and present the contexts and debates of the films themselves and the film culture of which they are a part' (p. 4).

The general context of the BFI Production Board films is that of the Independent Cinema in Britain. This movement involves film-makers, distributors, exhibitors, critics, theorists and the constituencies that use the films and developed independently of State funding and is represented in the U.K. both regionally and nationally by the Independent Filmmakers Association. Unable to raise sufficient exchange in the marketplace and no longer willing to run itself on unpaid labour, the recent history of the independent constituency is one of intervention in, and engagement with, the State institutions which fund the cinema in Britain. The most important of these has been the British Film Institute and the self-defined brief of its Production Board is to fund one-off productions—leaving the funding of the infrastructure of the independent sector (in the form of cinemas, workshops, documentation, publications, etc.) to other departments of the Institute, which in turn, delimit their own responsibilities.

The Production Board conceives of its functions as a producer of *films*, as opposed to, say, a 'promoter of film culture'. In other words, its defined task has a product-based orientation. Independent filmmakers, so persistently ghettoized by the large cinema chains and the TV industry (and thus made invisible to the 'general public'), have had to fight a series of battles around questions of audience, the uses of film in particular contexts, the development of new exhibition sites and so on. These battles have utilized our marginal status and turned it to our advantage. By consolidating a notion of practice based on work *with* audiences, film-makers, together with independent distributors and other sympathetic groups, are producing a kind of cinema which engages more concretely with specific issues.

It is with this background that the Production Board Catalogue must be read, for otherwise it presents a picture of independent film-makers in the U.K. which is not commensurate with the range of practices which are ongoing.

Elizabeth Cowie says in her introduction: 'The heterogeneity of the material included on each film reflects the diversity of the group of films, a group only inasmuch as they are all funded by the Production Board' (p. 4).

Whilst this is true, it is nonetheless also true that the crucially important moment of textual production occurs at the point at which meaning is constructed by the audience. In other words at the point of *use*, rather than simply of production. So the 'heterogeneity' of the films which is posed here has to be qualified by an analysis of the kind of relation to audience which it is possible for these films to have.

I would argue that the feminist films here form a significantly separate category inasmuch as they have an active engagement with specific audiences and events, which the other films, placed less flexibly in an 'art-house' context, find more difficult to achieve.

Anne Cottringer's essay, 'Representation and Feminist Film Practice' takes up the history of women's work in the cinema and specifies three ways in which women have been able to counter and criticize 'oppressive' forms of representation—'by entering the industry and trying to work within its limitations, by making films outside the commercial industrial system and by developing feminist film criticism' (p. 39). These different kinds of activity have traversed the women's movement (and educational practice) in such a way as to make it practically impossible to raise one issue (dominant cinema, independent cinema, feminist theory) without raising the other two by implication. Cottringer quotes Claire Johnston in 1973 envisaging a cinema where 'ideas from the entertainment film should inform the political film, the political ideas should inform the entertainment film: a two-way process.' A number of the films presented in the Catalogue do achieve this synthesis of concerns which necessarily commands them a feminist platform, a feminist audience.

Animation for Live Action (Vera Neubauer) attempts 'an engagement between film-maker and film, animator and animated, between the internal world of fantasy, imagination and desire and the external "reality" ' by cross-referencing live-action footage of the female animator with a kind of cartoon commentary.

Rapunzel Let Down Your Hair (Susan Shapiro, Esther Ronay, Francine Winham) provides a feminist interpretation of the Rapunzel fairy tale by means of engaging ironically with different 'dominant' styles—the detective story, the 'woman's weepie'—in the context of a didactic treatment of witchcraft and misogyny, done in an innovatory animated style. The film-makers, in their own account of the project, are conspicuously concerned with the way in which different devices work for specific audiences. They are faced with the problem that 'if we were to make a film about sexuality which had to appeal to the BFI Production Board, they probably wouldn't like a documentary about orgasms, they would probably like something slightly less "straightforward" '. However, while concerned to build up a more theoretical approach to the question of women's sexuality, their reference is always the usefulness of new cinematic devices to ongoing debates and struggles, rather than an abstract criterion of 'innovation' or 'progressiveness'.

It is primarily through the medium of audience discussion that feminist films like *Rapunzel, Riddles of the Sphinx, Animation for Live Action* and *Mirror Phase* can construct their meaning.

It is the film-makers' own statements which invariably carry the most credibility in this context, as their concern with audiences necessarily traverses the areas of aesthetics, finance and practical logistics, in a most interesting way. One of the most important departures at London's *Other Cinema* was a series of consecutive screenings of *Riddles of the Sphinx* (Mulvey and Wollen) each followed by a different debate—on childcare, psychoanalysis, etc. Thus the film's meaning was actively and variously constructed by audiences.

Sadly, however, the authorship which commands this kind of work and experience tends to be generally and critically associated with the more mythic and mystifying aspects of Authorship; that is to say, relying on the exponents of a film for an account of its effectivity places the kind of dependence on the authorial position which the new cinema has been precisely concerned to undercut. The solution to this would seem to be that the film writers and critics take up not only the question of films as 'texts' but also the context of audience, use and cultural operation.

The BFI Productions Catalogue represents the beginning of this kind of work and it is the women's films which have made the development of this kind of investigation not only viable but crucial to politically effective cinema.

SUE CLAYTON

MY SONG IS MY OWN by Kathy Henderson with Frankie Armstrong and Sandra Kerr, 188 pages. Pluto Press, London, 1979. Price £3.95.

SISTERS IN SONG by Tierl Thompson, Andrea Webb and Janie Faychild, 100 pages. Womens' Liberation Music Project, London, 1979. Price £2.50.

The first two British feminist song collections to be published turn out to have very different styles and approaches. It would be surprising if women's music remained untouched by the polarities of the women's movement, and the songbooks roughly reflect two different sorts of feminist thinking—although that hasn't stopped the editors from co-operating, for instance to cut down on duplication of material. Depending where you stand you may well love one book and be critical of the other, though I found them thoroughly complementary, in strengths and weaknesses as well as content.

At first sight *My Song is my Own* is a folk scholar's book, complete with references, footnotes and dialect translations. But do not despair! The excellent editors, probably fed up with ploughing through all those appendices at Cecil Sharp House, have presented the information simply and clearly right beside the songs. More importantly for the practical singer, the tunes and words are clearly set out and you need only rudimentary sight reading to use this book. It includes contemporary songs, but the emphasis is traditional. The four main sections, Love, Marriage, Motherhood/Childhood and Work, will probably get criticized for heterosexist bias; the editors say they 'were unable to find any gay womens' songs from this country that . . . stood up beside the rest'. I think they have misstated the problem slightly! there *are* good contemporary Lesbian songs but most of them don't have the stark chorus-and-verse simplicity to fit into a book that gives only a one-line tune and basic guitar chords.

I was dubious about some inclusions, for example 'Marrowbones', where the old husband gets the better of his wife. And 'Blow Away the Morning Dew', on the common folk theme of a woman getting her own back on a would-be sexual exploiter, has her telling him: 'If you will not when you may, you shall not when you would', i.e. she would think better of him if he *had* taken advantage of her when the going was good. I also missed some of my favourites like 'Tam Lin', where the mortal woman rescues the bewitched knight from the Elf Queen: a real change from knights rescuing ladies. But of course no collection will have everyone's favourites, and this one compensates with some real and little known gems, from the music hall ('If you want to scrape a boot, a safety razor blade is cute, so you must have a man about the house') and from children's street rhymes ('My Ma's a Millionaire'). And whatever its shortcomings it will be an invaluable source book for songs women have been hearing from singers like Frankie Armstrong and Peggy Seeger and now want to sing for themselves.

If *My Song is my Own* is an accessible book, *Sisters in Song* positively reaches out and invites women in. No assumptions about your musical knowledge here: this book undertakes to teach you to read and understand written music. The instruction sections do contain one or two errors that could be confusing, but on the whole they are remarkably effective, as well as beautifully set out in italic script with some excellent graphics.

All the songs here are contemporary, and this poses quite different problems. If we want 'political' songs we often have to struggle with obstinately antilyrical words and ideas: how on earth do you fit 'capitalism' or 'sexuality' into a song? The answer is, usually, you squash it in sideways and have to put up with all but the most right-on singers making faces or collapsing in giggles when they get to *that* bit. This is my one serious quarrel with the book: we're expected to sing, presumably with a straight face, things like 'Keep on examining your sexuality' or 'That don't eradicate our conditioning' (I was irresistibly reminded of having to sing the full text of 'O Come All ye Faithful' at school, including 'Lo, He ab–hor–rs not the Vir–r–gins Womb'!!). But this, after all, is only part of the process of sifting and refinement that any raw, new culture must go through, and for every unsingable line there are several of unsurpassed elegance, most of which I cannot do justice to by quoting; except maybe to show the truly funny things that *can* be done with unwieldy words: 'Queen Victoria didn't think we even went together, Ladies, but, bent together, Ladies, we're content!' A–men!

BARBARA NORDEN

INDEX